I0485173

Computer Factoids

Computer Factoids

✦

tales from the high-tech underbelly

Kirk Kirksey

iUniverse, Inc.
New York Lincoln Shanghai

Computer Factoids
tales from the high-tech underbelly

Copyright © 2005 by Kirk Kirksey

All rights reserved. No part of this book may be used or reproduced by any means, graphic, electronic, or mechanical, including photocopying, recording, taping or by any information storage retrieval system without the written permission of the publisher except in the case of brief quotations embodied in critical articles and reviews.

iUniverse books may be ordered through booksellers or by contacting:

iUniverse
2021 Pine Lake Road, Suite 100
Lincoln, NE 68512
www.iuniverse.com
1-800-Authors (1-800-288-4677)

ISBN-13: 978-0-595-31891-9 (pbk)
ISBN-13: 978-0-595-66440-5 (cloth)
ISBN-13: 978-0-595-76699-4 (ebk)
ISBN-10: 0-595-31891-6 (pbk)
ISBN-10: 0-595-66440-7 (cloth)
ISBN-10: 0-595-76699-4 (ebk)

Printed in the United States of America

For

Aaron and Sarah

and

For J.P.

Maybe this book
would have made you smile.

factoid, *n. and a*
A. *n. Something that becomes accepted as a fact, although it is not (or may not be) true; spec. an assumption or speculation reported and repeated so often that it is popularly considered true; a simulated or imagined fact.*

—The Oxford English Dictionary

fac·toid
1 : an invented fact believed to be true because of its appearance in print
2 : a brief and usually trivial news item

—Merriam Webster Dictionary

fac·toid
A piece of unverified or inaccurate information that is presented in the press as factual, often as part of a publicity effort, and that is then accepted as true because of frequent repetition. A brief, somewhat interesting fact.

—The American Heritage Dictionary of the English Language

Contents

Introduction

Computers are no laughing matter. They invade our lives, try our patience, and obliterate our book manuscripts for no good reason. On the other hand, computers and the people who run them can do some mighty silly things. Twenty five years ago I learned how the smallest error in computer software can turn order and symmetry into a farce. You see, in those days, I was the young computer programmer at a large medical center, eager to make my mark. One of my first assignments involved setting up appointments for a large number of patients. With boastful pride, the project was finished ahead of schedule. Unfortunately, I had programmed a small "bug" in the software, and several hundred male patients were scheduled to receive a routine gynecological exam. The incident is still talked about today.

Merciless humiliation carved out a special place in my heart for high-tech oddities and *Computer Factoids* was born. It didn't take long to discover a prolific underground of digital mythology. In the early eighties I heard stories of a janitor's vacuum cleaner causing the crash of a multi-million dollar computer center. At a computer conference in San Diego, engineers played a tape of eerie Christmas carols. IBM technicians had found a way to make a high-speed line printer play "Oh Come All Ye Faithful." Then there was the story of hacker legend John Drapper, a.k.a. Cap'n Crunch. Draper used a giveaway whistle from a popular breakfast cereal to fool AT&T computers and bamboozled Ma Bell out of long distance services worth thousands of dollars. Computers, it seems, can be a laughing matter after all.

As the years passed, I amassed a large collection of computer history, lore, legend, and rumor. In 1998 I introduced a one-line *computer factoid* at the end of my *Back to Basics* column published in a California computer magazine. I began receiving more email about my *factoids* than the technical subjects I covered in my column. People, I discovered, loved the quirky side of technology. I expanded *Computer Factoid* into a full-fledged column carried by technology magazines in Texas, California, and Illinois. I interviewed a man who powered a computer with rotting potatoes; listened to a symphony composed for dot matrix printers; and learned to GoogleWhack. On the pages of *Computer Factoids*, the book, you will find the best of the best; the weirdest of the weird; the silliest computer stories of all times. No punches are pulled, no quarter is given, and attitude is everything.

There are those who will criticize this book for not following rigorous journalistic standards (I have probably received nasty email from most of these people already). They are correct, hence the use of *factoid* in the title. The word was invented by Norman Mailer in his 1973 biography of Marilyn Monroe. Definitions vary, but *factoid* generally has come to mean a trivial fact or a snippet of information. Sometimes the snippet is true. Other times the material cannot be substantiated. When it comes to shenanigans involving computers, most organizations aren't enthusiastic about airing their dirty high-tech laundry. Computer experts are quick to ridicule their colleagues, but almost never reveal their own *factoids*. Doing so would blow their cover. I have interviewed participants and reviewed official documents for many of the *factoids* in this book. Other stories, I must admit, are based on rumor, legend, lore, or a blend of all three.

You may think these stories are no more than bits of outlandish trivia good for nothing better than passing the time on an uncomfortable plane ride. Perhaps. But mark my words; someday you will receive a computer-generated form informing you of your own death or a $4,578,241.73 water bill. When it happens, think about this little book because dear reader, you have just entered the strange and bizarre world of *Computer Factoids*.

Kirk Kirksey
Dallas, Texas

COMPUTER FACTOID

fac · toid \fak' toid"\'   *n:*a single fact
or statistic variously regarded as being
trivial, useless, unsubstantiated, etc.

The Windows 95 Startup Sound

For years, Microsoft dreamed of clobbering archrival Apple Computer. In the mid-nineties Gates and company got their chance. After four profitable quarters, Apple's market share tumbled, and the company was bleeding money. Mac zealots grew tired of waiting for Apple's new Version 8 operating system. The product was already twelve months behind schedule and dangerously over budget. Deserters switched to PC-based Lotus for integrated spreadsheets and word processing. Microsoft saw it all coming and moved in for the kill. A brand new operating system for the PC would be the battleground. Windows 95 became the epicenter of a global media blitz positioned to overshadow everything from war in Somalia to the Second Coming.

In an unprecedented move, Gates paid the Rolling Stones $10 million and transformed Mick Jagger's 1981 anthem of nasty passion into the pansified theme song of the Windows 95 'Start Me Up' campaign. Behind the scenes, another musical milestone—the creation of the Windows 95 Startup Sound—went unnoticed.

Out with the Old

From the beginning, the old Windows startup procedure had been saddled with the irritating bell tones. Angry customers took the sound and created tasteless epithets describing Microsoft's buggy Windows 3.1 operating system. After receiving an unexpected error, some users were fond of saying, "Windows just tinkled on me." Folks in Redmond weren't happy and wanted a new sound. They needed a professional.

Microsoft's PR machine contacted musician Brian Eno through a third party. Early in his career, Eno played the synthesizer for the alternative rock band Roxy

Music. Since leaving Roxy, Eno had invented a genre he dubbed Ambient Music—an offshoot of something called Furniture Music dreamed up by French modernist Erik Satie around the turn of the century. Ambient Music and its granddaddy Furniture are hard to describe (aficionados think Furniture Music is supposed to be present, but not listened to). Music writer Malcolm Humes describes Eno's Ambient style as "...something that is quiet, sparse and perhaps gentle; using silence and textures more to achieve a mood more than via melody, meters or arrangements of instruments. Reading between the lines of Humes commentary, one correctly concludes an Eno tune is hard to hum.

Eno, a compulsive recluse, began work on the Windows assignment after receiving instructions through a musical agency. According to Eno in a 1996 interview, Microsoft wanted him to write a snippet of sound "...that is inspiring, universal, optimistic, futuristic, sentimental, emotional, blah, blah blah—this whole list of adjectives." Seemed easy enough, and then came the kicker. The composition could only be 3.25 to 4 seconds long. Over a period of four months, Eno produced eighty-four possibilities. In the end he settled on a synthesized arpeggio ascending in tone and volume that drifted into a singular repeating note before fading away—all in less than 4 seconds. Eno delivered his 'Startup Sound' to Microsoft sometime in early 1995 and the rest, so they say, is history.

(Windows 95 Sound courtesy of Microsoft)

How Much?

When the Windows 95 dust settled, Jagger and the Stones drove away with a boatload of cash for the partial replay of a track from "Tattoo You", an album released in 1981. What was Eno's take for his four-second composition? No one is talking about his financial arrangement with Microsoft, but possibilities make for interesting speculation. Many experts say the Windows startup sound is the shortest piece of music ever commissioned, and some believe Eno's creation has been heard by more people than any other composition in history. Let's talk money.

Most musicians get a royalty payment each time their work is played. If Microsoft pays royalties each time the Windows 95 sound is played, Eno probably has more money than Bill Gates himself. Not likely. Chances are Microsoft paid Eno a flat fee for his work. If this is the case, you can bet his fee hit stratospheric heights.

There is one final twist to the story. In 1996, Eno published portions of his journal called *A Year with Swollen Appendices* (Faber and Faber). He briefly mentions the use of an Apple computer in his work. One Eno Site Webmaster told this author that Eno also uses Tom Bender's Tex-Edit to spark musical creativity. Tex-Edit is shareware written for Apple computers. For Mac zealots, Eno's diary and the Tex-Edit rumor are more than enough ammo for the ultimate Microsoft slam. Brian Eno probably created the Windows 95 startup sound on a Macintosh computer.

Ouch.

fac · toid \fak' toid'\'   *n:* a single fact
or statistic variously regarded as being
trivial, useless, unsubstantiated, etc.

Keyboard Crud

Pick up your computer keyboard, turn it over, and shake vigorously over a sheet of clean, white paper. Try popping off a couple of keys if you're compelled to do a thorough job. In computer slang, the resultant fallout is called *Party Mix*. Examine said *Party Mix* closely. You are likely to find a pile of unidentified crumbs, dandruff flakes, maybe a drop of brown ooze, and a hair or two. Disgusting, and who the heck cares anyway? Domino's Pizza and communications behemoth AOL, that's who. Here's how the AOL/Domino's keyboard crud research study went down.

Crud Beneath My Keys

At the height of the Dot Com insanity, Domino's needed a new scam for pushing the nation's cholesterol and waistlines to even greater heights. Stats from companies like PricewaterhouseCoopers™ showed Internet surfing was becoming Americans' leisure activity of choice, edging out boob tube watching and (gulp) reading. This begged the obvious question. What are all these people going to eat while they thump on their keyboards? No doubt an erudite Domino's pizza executive put two and two together one weekend while languishing in his hot tub. The answer was obvious; ePizza, the perfect geek food. The pizza giant would partner with AOL to create an Internet-based ordering and payment system. For Web addicts, Nirvana was at hand. Netizans would be able to order pizza online, then pay with a credit card. The only exertion required was walking a few feet when the doorbell rang and sorting out the paper plates. In theory, ePizza sounded promising. But before investing zillions, Dominos and AOL needed to answer one very important question. Does the typical Internet slob dine while sitting at his or her computer? Here's where keyboard crud comes in.

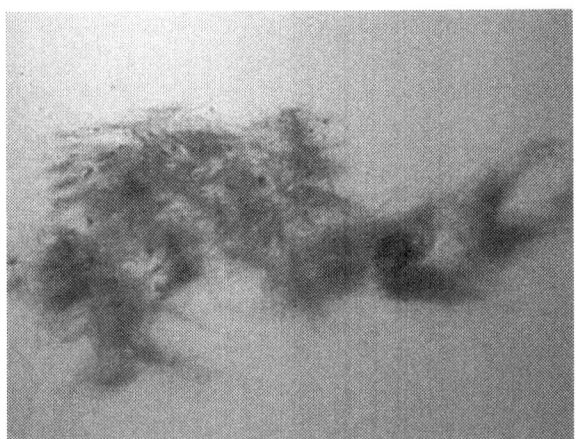

Party Mix or Keyboard Crud
(Image courtesy of Jeff Covey)

Domino's wanted to field test the ePizza program in England. If you've ever eaten British food (baked cow innards wrongly called 'pie'), you know why. Limeys are desperate for something tasty. Anyway, AOL came up with a plan to scientifically analyze keyboard crud. If they found food, ePizza was on its way.

A food-and-drink consulting outfit called Reading Scientific Services (www.rssl.co.uk) was commissioned to carry out the study. Every day, two unidentified London companies sent samples of keyboard crud to Reading's lab. This went on, if you can believe it, for a month.

All in all, the accumulated payload from a single keyboard weighed about two grams. If these numbers are true, a bit of elementary arithmetic indicates United Kingdom keyboards catch over one-half ton of keyboard crud in a typical year. On a global scale, the annual grunge accumulation would fill over five hundred double loader garbage trucks. That's about 37.5 million tons. What's more surprising than the tonnage is the composition of the detritus shaken from the typical British keyboard.

Food particles made up over 50% of keyboard crud, with 15% attributed to corn flakes, and another 15% reported to be 'boiled sweet', a British approximation of candy. Seven percent (7%) was noodles. Unnamed vegetable bits (I'm betting these were brussel sprouts) tailed the food category with 4%. Biscuit (that's cookie to you and me), bread, pastry crumbs, and chocolate specks filled in the remainder of the food category. One conclusion is striking. Keyboard crud is mostly edible. AOL and Domino's had struck pay dirt. Geeks eat a lot of stuff while sitting at their computers. Why not pizza?

Outside the food category, a three-way tie for the 1% spot went to leaf bits, staples, and pencil shavings. Fingernails, tape, insects, foil, and hair were clocked at less than 1%. There you have it.

But is it Safe?

Keyboard crud news didn't make much of a splash in the tech press, but many of those who did hear about the study pressed for a statement about the dangers of the so called Party Mix. In well-crafted dribble, spin doctors from Reading Scientific Software said they would not comment on the health hazards of the stuff. In the spirit of hard-driving investigative reporting, I decided to doggedly pursue the health angle. I emailed Reading Scientific and requested complete study results. Someone responded saying they didn't really believe I was Peter Jennings, and all of this was none of my business anyway. Next, I emailed and even called AOL offices. Same story different day. At this point I had exhausted my enormous research budget for this factoid and gave up. Still, all of this secrecy surrounding keyboard crud seems very fishy to me. I'm hoping Saddam Hussein didn't stockpile any of this stuff.

There you have it. Details of the Keyboard Crud Study were covered up by the Brits. Domino's started the ePizza online ordering craze, AOL gets a piece of the pie, and Americans are fatter than ever.

The Crud Conspiracy

Keyboard crud is gross. It is everywhere, and it isn't going away. I'm not sure we even know the full extent of the problem. An informal poll of help desk techs at my office elicited rolled eyes and some pretty interesting stories. According to my unnamed sources, "There is more than cookie crumbs and noodle bits in a typical user's keyboard."

Before someone finds something incriminating, you may want to vacuum and clean your keyboard regularly just like the manual recommends. But who's got time? A better solution may be a doohickey manufactured by iNPACE, "The Keyboard Glove," www.inpace.com. They call it the Keyboard Glove, but Keyboard Condom might be a more accurate name. The Keyboard Glove is a piece of flexible polyurethane that wraps around the keyboard. In their ad, a hand can be seen pouring coffee on a keyboard without effect. I'm assuming the Keyboard Glove will also protect the keyboard from cookie crumbs, boiled sweets, fingernails, and pepperoni juice. By the way, Domino's cash registers use the Glove, and iPACE is a British company. I am certain some sort of conspiracy is involved.

I'm not sure what to make of the keyboard crud study. Maybe this is one of those arcane bits of knowledge someone will find useful in a hundred years. Maybe not. I do know AOL spent real money to study keyboard crud. I wish they had fixed their stupid browser instead.

Computer Factoid

fac · toid \fak' toid'\' *n*:a single fact or statistic variously regarded as being trivial, useless, unsubstantiated, etc.

Computers in the Tabloids

Not long ago I was standing in the checkout line behind a large woman and three penitentiary escapees posing as her children. I was feeling a tad despondent when something on the tabloid rack caught my eye. It was a headline in the *Weekly World News*, "3 Breasted Gal Joins Clinton as His New Intern." There was even a picture. Lusting for the rest of the story I grabbed my very own copy. By the time my celery and I reached the cash register, I had read the WWN cover-to-cover. Did you know researchers have found a space alien implant in Jennifer Lopez's heinie? And that human brains are being transplanted into racehorses by a Saudi sheikh? How's this for a scoop—an unnamed NBA team is about to sign a nine-foot Cyclops. Why doesn't CNN know about this stuff?

If the *Weekly World News* can sniff out stories about JL's butt and Clinton's three-boobed aide, they must know something about the latest high-tech developments. This *is* the Information Age, for gosh sakes. I began a quest for the top five high-tech stories as reported by that pillar of journalistic integrity, the *Weekly World News*.

Rules

Lest you think the winners were selected just because the WWN article contained the word 'computer' or 'internet,' think again. This thing has rules.

First, the story has got to be completely idiotic. Any hint of rational thinking or accuracy and the entry was immediately disqualified. For example, one WWN writer actually knew what the initials DSL stood for. His story was out of the running.

Second, not a single fact in the article could be corroborated with an independent source. Names and places (other than big cities and celebrities of course) presented as facts had to be completely spurious. If a cited organization was found to actually exist, or the name of a quoted "expert" showed up in an online white pages directory, the story wasn't even considered.

Last, but not least, the article had to have something to do with computers or information technology; the more technology, the higher the score.

For those who haven't already spread the pages of this book in the bottom of your parakeet's cage, here are the Top Five Information Technology Stories from the *Weekly World News*.

NUMBER FIVE...

"Washington Think Tanks are
Riddled with Space Aliens"
(5 March 2001)

Did you ever wonder why all those ideas from places like the Brookings Institute seem so out-of-this-world? It's simple—every think tank in Washington employs at least one space alien. No joke. Some even have five. After twenty-three years with the prestigious Holt-Ventman Institute, Dr. Berhard Galtham broke his vow of silence and spilled his guts. Extraterrestrials are recruited from a small planet orbiting Sirius B. They are slightly built, have large, slanted eyes, and attend all the meetings. According to Dr. Galtham, space aliens have been the driving force behind some pretty high-profile projects. There's the polio vaccine, the Apollo space program, and—you guessed it—the Internet.

NUMBER FOUR...

"Demon Computer Kills Two Workers
Exorcist Called In After Experts Discover Virus Bred Evil Spirit"
(12 November 1991)

Two employees of a bank in Valparaiso, Chile were murdered by a horned demon living inside a computer terminal. One woman was found with her head in her lap. An associate suffered a heart attack two minutes after sitting down to work. Things turned from bad to worse when computer experts tried to examine the computer. One of them started babbling like a madman while others were flung to the ground by an unseen force. "We can't turn the machine off," said one official, "because everyone who tries, blacks out and falls to the floor." A bank custodian reported seeing a hideous horned devil on the screen. Later an official from the firm hired to install the machine attributed the possession to some sort of computer virus gone haywire. Father Hector Diaz, a local priest, was called to banish the spirit from the possessed computer, but admitted he did not know if the problem was in the boot sector or an email attachment. Regardless of the demon's composition, bank officials agreed. If Father Diaz's exorcism failed, the bank would have to be closed.

NUMBER THREE…

"Secret Government Plot to Implant Biochips in
Every Man, Woman and Child"
(27 March 2001)

Looks like Beelzebub has pulled a fast one on the U.S. government. To prove it, fundamentalist researcher Terry Cook, from parts unnamed, cites Revelation 13:16—"He (the Anti-Christ) causeth all, both small and great, rich and poor, free and bond, to receive a mark in their right hand or in their forehead. And that no man might buy or sell, save he that had the mark." What could it be? Tattoo? Birthmark? Malformed hair follicle? None of the above is Cook's guess. He says it's a glass-encased biochip transponder that's already being used in pets. "Heck," says Cook, "if it's working in Fido, why not put it in Freddy." The feds claim the chip will carry vital medical and identity information, but Cook thinks the government story is full of hooey. He says the biochip implant is the work of the devil. The Prince of Darkness (possibly in cahoots with WalMart) really plans to use the chip to enslave mankind. Only those with the chip will be allowed to buy and sell. Anybody else will be hunted down like a dog.

NUMBER TWO…

"Hackers Can Make Your PC Explode"
(Author's Note: This story was attributed to the *Weekly World News* but posted by the British tabloid, *The Register*, on 4 July 2000. It is still stupid as heck.)

If you thought Melissa or Code Red were bad, check this out. Arnold Yabenson, president of the Washington-based consumer group National CyberCrime Prevention Foundation (NCPF), says we've only seen the tip of the iceberg. Hackers are dreaming up stuff your average computer expert can't even imagine. They're about to crack a secret code that will unleash Russky missiles on the US, and can make airplanes explode in mid—air. Here's the worst part—Yabenson says hackers can now send an email attachment capable of altering the molecular and electronic structure of the family PC. Bottom line—Junior opens the wrong email attachment and the whole family is blown to smithereens.

Drum roll, please.

And the NUMBER ONE, most asinine story about technology from *The Weekly World News* is…

"Is Your Computer Possessed by a Demon?"
(12 March 2000)

Savannah pastor the most Reverend Jim Peasboro, author of the soon-to-be-published *The Devil in the Machine* (publisher unnamed), noticed members of his flock acting a little strangely. "I learned some people in my congregation came in touch with a dark force whenever they used their computers," says Peasboro. He was surprised to learn married men were looking at dirty pictures on the Web, and housewives were using naughty language in chat rooms. Could this be true? According to the story, Peasboro investigated the phenomenon by actually logging on to a parishioner's computer. When he did, the device went haywire and started printing out gobbledygook. Turns out the printout was a stream of obscenities written in a 2,800-year-old Mesopotamian dialect.

After exhaustive research, here's what Peasboro learned. Any PC built after 1985 has the hard disk capacity to house a demon from hell. This means one in ten computers in America is possessed. Exorcism won't work. If you suspect your computer is possessed you should have a skilled technician replace the hard drive and reload the software. I'd stay away from Windows XP if I were you.

FLASH—THIS JUST IN

Bizarre Virus Turns Computer into Sex Pervert
(September 23, 2003)

Stockholm—It seems a group of comely coeds at Stockholm University installed a Web cam on their dorm room computer. They were shocked to learn their nude photos were being posted on Internet sites. At first they thought their boyfriends were playing a little joke. Au contraire. Authorities soon learned the girls' computer developed a sort of rudimentary artificial intelligence and had created its own pornographic Web site. Computer expert Dr. Niles Sanksuson says,

"During our examination what boggled our mind was that we were able to communicate—talk if you will—with the machine. It denied the whole thing." According to Dr. Sanksuson, "I can only theorize that somehow, a new computer virus combined with a new operating system software to, in effect, bring this computer to life, with a consciousness not unlike our own." Experts who continue examining the computer say the machine should be 'hailed, not jailed.'

Your *Computer Factoid* reporter has looked into some might weird stuff, mighty weird indeed. But the *Weekly World News*—now that's reporting. Pick one up today.

fac · toid \fak' toid'\' *n:* a single fact
or statistic variously regarded as being
trivial, useless, unsubstantiated, etc.

Cheeseburgers, Cyberspace, and Immortality

In 1993 Joseph Paul Jernigan, a thirty-nine-year-old convicted murderer, had been on Texas Death Row for twelve years. During the summer he lost a final appeal for clemency. On August 5, Jernigan ate his last meal—a couple of cheeseburgers, French fries, and iced tea. At 12:31 A.M., he was executed by a lethal injection of potassium chloride. End of story? Not by a long shot. Today you may run into Jernigan in a junior high science class or a medical school anatomy lecture or even at the movies. Even though death came for Jernigan that night in Huntsville, Texas, digital technology resurrected his body. This Texas murderer has gone virtual. Our story begins seven years before Jernigan walked into the execution chamber.

In 1986 the Internet was a toddler, 300 baud was blazing, and 'portables' weighed as much a small car. Despite technology limitations of the day, executives at the National Library of Medicine (NLM) had their eyes on the future. Electronic images would become increasingly important for medical education, clinical practice, and biomedical research. This meant vast amounts of digital information must be delivered over high-speed networks to very large computers. An extensive period of planning began, and in 1989 a special panel recommended, "building a digital image library of volumetric data representing a complete, normal adult male and female." TRANSLATION: Experts wanted to digitize the dead body of a human being. The Visible Human project was born. Dr. Micheal Ackerman, a young biomedical engineer at NLM, was assigned the task of making it happen.

Not Just Any Body

Up to now, only digital images of body parts had been available for researchers and educators. Ackerman's goal was to produce an entire digital cadaver. This wouldn't be easy. The first problem was the state of computer technology in the late eighties. Experts estimated the digitization of a complete cadaver would require 10 to 20 gigabytes of storage. Way back then, 20 gig was lot of very expensive disk space. And if storage wasn't a big enough problem, the processing power needed to manipulate such a humongous data set was no where to be found. Hollywood came to the rescue. As the legend goes, an unnamed studio executive who was watching computers take over the world of special effects counseled Dr. Ackerman. His advice to the young scientist was prophetic. Build the Visible Human, and computer power would catch up. Ackerman decided to gamble on the future.

The first thing Dr. Ackerman needed was a body—not an easy assignment since the project required a normal male, under 6 feet tall, and between 21 and 60 years of age. Under 6 feet—OK. Between 21 and 60—no problem. But normal? Most men between the ages of 21 and 60 who die, die of something ugly. Car wrecks cause nasty trauma; heart attacks blow out the vascular plumbing. Strokes toast gray matter. Gunshots leave unsightly holes. The Visible Human Project needed a body that was not damaged by accident, malfeasance, or disease. The answer came from a Texas prison chaplain who convinced several condemned men, including Joseph Paul Jernigan, to donate their bodies to science. Dr. Ackerman's team had an answer.

Seven hours after the execution, Jernigan's body was flown to a lab at the University of Colorado where a thorough examination was performed. Results were promising. Even though Jernigan was missing a tooth, a testicle, and an appendix, Ackerman's team determined they had found their Visible Man. The process of digitizing Jernigan's anatomy could begin. Dr. Victor Spitzer, a professor in the University of Colorado's Department of Cellular and Structural Biology, went to work. If you've got a weak stomach, STOP READING NOW.

Sawing for Science

Steps required to create the Visible Man easily remind one of a B—horror movie gorefest, so don't forget; this is science. Here's how it worked. Dr. Spitzer's team would slice off a microscopic layer of Jernigan's body, then take Magnetic Resonance Imaging (MRI) and CTI images looking down on the newly-exposed portion of the cadaver. The result was something kin to a very large stack of digital pancakes. The slicing/imaging process continued until nothing was left of Jernigan's body. Once complete, the MRI and CTI images would be digitized and restacked on a computer.

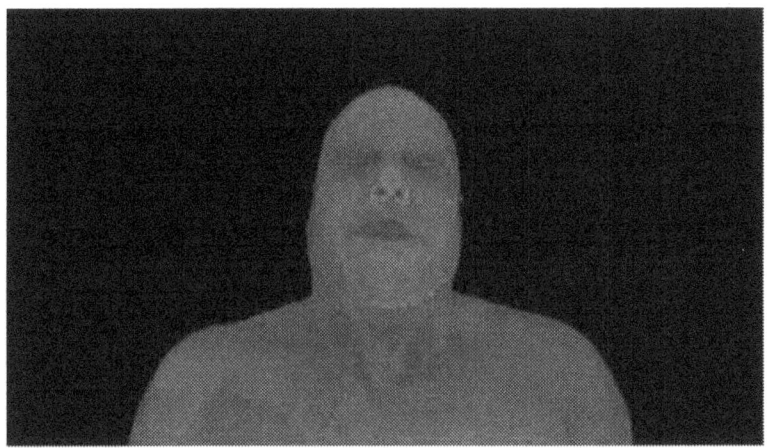

Richard Jernigan as the Visible Man
(Image courtesy of the National Library of Medicine)

Spizter knew stability of the body was the key to success. His team only had one shot. If the body shifted during the sawing process, slices would be off kilter and the MRI images would be misaligned. The body could not move, even slightly, during the process. Gooey latex was pumped into Jernigan's hollow body cavities and the entire cadaver was frozen at about 95 degrees below zero for two days. The icy block was cut into four chunks. Spitzer packed the pieces in—get this—Jello obtained from the University's cafeteria (think about that the next time you're about to dig into your granny's lime Jello salad). The tedious process of photographing the Visible Man began in February 1994.

Spitzer's team used a special circular saw sort of like one of those electric deli knives that shave off microscopic slices of smoked turkey. He started at the feet, taking off slices measuring no more than one millimeter thick. Visit http:// www.nlm.nih.gov/research/visible/image/feet_fresh.jpg and you can clearly see the toe bones in each foot. After each slice, technicians prepared the surface and a CT scan was used to photograph the axial section. The block was refrozen, and the slicing and scanning process was repeated. When the team reached the head and neck, MRI shots were taken at 4mm intervals. At first, the team worked twelve hours a day, but cut back to six shifts during the summer when air conditioning became a problem. In September 1994, Spitzer and his team had photographed over 18,000 slices. The digitized version of the Visible Man was 15 gigabytes and in 1994 filled 15,000 diskettes.

The data set for the visible man is around 15 megabytes, and is available at the National Library of Medicine Web site. You can find Joseph Paul Jernigan and his bad virtual self at <u>http://www.nlm.nih.gov/research/visible/visible_human.html</u>. In addition to the public domain data set, the project has spawned a number of teaching products, aids, and animations.

ADDENDUM: Using the cadaver of an anonymous "housewife" from Maryland, the Visible Female project was completed in November 1995.

COMPUTER FACTOID

fac · toid \fak' toid'\'   *n*:a single fact
or statistic variously regarded as being
trivial, useless, unsubstantiated, etc.

Age-Old Beer Mystery Solved

Once in a blue moon along comes a breakthrough—a thing so revolutionary its value can only be measured by the complexity of problems it is called on to solve. So it is with Hannibal's elephants; Einstein's Theory of Relativity, and with Dr. Clive Fletcher and New Hampshire-based Fluent Software.

From the corporate Web site the Fluent product is unassuming, almost pathetic; like a mutt looking for an owner. Oh sure, the customer list is respectable with the likes of the Department of Energy, Shell, and Mitsubishi. You see, Fluent is engineering software designed to simulate flow—flow of water, flow of air, flow of particles. For those of us who don't repair our eyeglasses with duct tape, flow analysis is boring stuff. Boring, but for one fact. In 1999, Dr. Fletcher, an Australian engineering professor, used Fluent Software to solve a problem that has plagued humankind for well over two hundred fifty years. The project involved beer.

The Guinness Legend

To connoisseurs of fine ales and beer, Guinness Stout, like gravity or expensive divorce lawyers, is simply a given. If you are a teetotaler or only emerge from your cave to buy this book, I can only say, Guinness is the finest brew in the world—period. It is nothing less than a liquid work of art. Brewed in Ireland for over two hundred fifty years, it is black in color with a luxurious, some even say creamy, tan head. Each of the nineteen variants, including Guinness Stout, Extra Stout, All Malt, etc., is blessed with a unique bite easily recognizable by brewski aficionados around the globe. I could go on, but I'd only end up with tears in my eyes.

Guinness taste is one thing, lads and lasses, but the Guinness legend is quite another kettle of fish. Throughout history, an ever-growing body of myth and folklore has surrounded this magnificent elixir. Coors Light should be so lucky. At one time, a pint of Guinness was given to hospital patients in Britain to replenish lost vitamins (Vitamin G—get it?). Today, the Black and Tan is still given to blood donors in Ireland. Old timers say you can tell a man's nationality by the number of rings left in his empty Guinness glass. Each swig leaves a ring of foam showing the previous volume. An Irishman will leave six rings, an American seventeen rings, and an Aussie won't leave any rings at all, finishing a pint in one gulp. But of all Guinness legends, the mystery of wrong-way bubbles is one of the oldest and most perplexing.

Phunny Physics

Alistair, a Newcastle bloke who perpetually occupied a stool in a London pub-slash-disco called the Brown Eyed Girl, first introduced this writer to Guinness Bubbles. The one thing Alistair loved more than his Black and Tan was swindling unsuspecting Yanks out of a fiver. His hustle went something like this. After a few minutes of disarming conversation, he would softly ask, "Did you know, mate, not all beer bubbles float up?" In fact, Alistair said certain bubbles in a glass of Guinness could clearly be seen sinking down toward the bottom of the glass. Only the Queen's currency, either wager or payment straight away, could coerce the limey to demonstrate this phenomenon.

With all bets in, Alistair would stroll behind the bar and draw Guinness Stout into one of those clear draught glasses shaped like a well-fed grandmother. Foam, fed by a parade of large upward-floating bubbles, formed a creamy head. But wait. Alistair pointed to the side of the glass. Sure enough, streams of tiny bubbles from the foam head could clearly be seen traveling down toward the bottom of the glass.

How could this be? Air pockets surrounded by the liquid substance in which they were formed must move upward. Even Archimedes, math nerd from ancient Greece, knew gas bubbles were lighter than their surrounding liquid, and must experience buoyancy. In other words, bubbles float up, not down. It's mandatory. Anything else is as silly as the Girl Scouts selling martinis instead of Do-Si-Dos. What could it all mean?

As it turns out, the wrong-way-bubbles-in-pint-of-Guinness problem has been a topic of speculation in pubs across the British Commonwealth for gosh-knows-how-long. Explanations range from hemispheric (bubbles act normal at Antarctica) to mystic (the tiniest bubbles flowing downward is the Almighty reminding us small minds are drawn downward to the devil) to stupid (those are really metal shavings painted to look like bubbles). It was all just speculation until Dr. Fletcher came along.

Going Down Under

In 1999, Professor Clive Fletcher from the University of New South Wales in Sydney, Australia, tackled the problem. Dr. Fletcher and a small band of dedicated graduate students began by observing, first-hand, countless glasses of freshly-poured Guinness in their favorite pub. "It was tough duty," reported one student.

Fletcher's rigorous observations proved a dead end, and the group was unable to uncover the secret. After drinking about all the Guinness they could stomach, the dedicated band of academics decided to construct a series of mathematical models using principles of computational flow dynamics. Computer simulation was in order, but they needed a software program. Fletcher chose the best computer modeling product on the market—Fluent Software, created right here in the good ole U.S of A.

Billed as flow and heat modeling software, Fluent takes in the specifics of a particular flow problem and spits out a model of, say, motor oil flowing through the moving parts of an engine. Engineers evaluate this stuff to cut down on drag thus increase the efficiency of anything moving in gas or liquids. Using Fluent, Fletcher first wanted a mathematical model of a pint glass, the kind typically found in British pubs. A series of mathematical equations would mimic the flow of Guinness into the glass at different angles and velocities. Employing known principles of physics built into the Fluent product, the software would construct patterns of flow inside the glass. When it was all said and done, Fletcher hoped to have a mathematical picture of swirling currents of ale, and the answer to the age-old, wrong-way bubbles question.

This problem of sinking bubbles is not an easy problem to solve. "It is incredibly complex to set up the computational model," says Dr. Fletcher. "Modeling the flow of an air conditioner or the dispersal of poisonous gas from a heating unit would be extremely simple in comparison." The shape of the Guinness pint glass must be meticulously measured and defined mathematically. There is the density and viscosity of the ale. Equations and formulae allowing for temperature must be created. And what about the bubbles themselves? Does size make a difference? Do large bubbles act differently than small ones? The simulation could only begin after these variables and more were translated into their mathematical equivalents, and plugged onto the Fluent software. Once the footwork was done, Dr. Fletcher and his students began their quest. In the end, Dr. Fletcher hoped to put the case of the descending bubbles to bed once and for all. So what's the answer?

Archimedes Who?

Fletcher got what he was after, and I'm happy to report that supernatural beings and metal shavings are not involved. Thanks to Fluent CFD, the answer is surprisingly simple. Here's how it works:

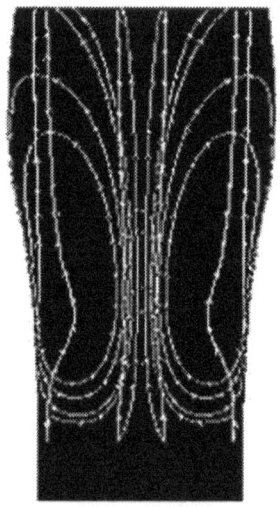

Flow Lines in a Guinness Pint
(Image courtesy of Fluent Software)

When the Guinness hits the glass, the motion forms a sort of swirling vortex creating bubbles of all sizes. Got the picture? Bubbles being bubbles, they all start to rise. However, bubbles near the center of the glass rise faster. As they rise, bubbles in the middle of the glass drag molecules of Guinness up too. Physics 101 teaches that overall mass must be preserved. So, the upward moving molecules must eventually move outward towards the glass boundary, then fall back toward the bottom of the glass in order to obey the aforementioned law and not get arrested by the Physics Police. Here comes the important part. Like upward-flowing bubbles, downward-traveling molecules of Guinness also create drag. This drag tries to pull surrounding bubbles downward. Large bubbles have enough mass to resist the force. However, bubbles with less than .05mm diameter (that's 0.002 of an inch) do not have enough buoyancy and do, in fact, "float" downwards along the edge of the glass. These are the wrong-way bubbles that pub-based philosophers, thinkers, swindlers, and drunks have pondered for over two hundred fifty years. Why don't we see bubbles float downward in a glass of Miller or Corona? Because, according to Dr. Fletcher, the unique viscosity of Guinness produces an overabundance of small bubbles.

Does the answer to the Guinness Bubbles have any practical application? Who knows? But if you ever find yourself sitting next to a Newcastle bloke in a London pub, and the conversation turns to bubbles in a glass of Stout, hang on to your fiver and buy yourself another pint of Black and Tan.

COMPUTER FACTOID

fac · toid \fak' toid'\'   *n*:a single fact or statistic variously regarded as being trivial, useless, unsubstantiated, etc.

SoftRAM—Software that Never Was

Shrinks call the condition cognitive dissonance. It's easy to spot.

Your brother-in-law forks over beaucoup dinero for a bag-o-bolts disguised as a Chevy then swears it's the best car made since the '74 Pinto.

It's been six weeks since your cousin moved in with a parolee from the Joliet Women's Unit and swears that he's happy. He got his broken nose and black eye when he fell down playing tennis at the club; really.

After thirty-six consecutive hours spent upgrading to Windows 2000 your spreadsheets disappeared into the ether. Must be the power lines behind the house.

'Marriage'—nuff said.

If you're thinking 'rationalization', 'gullibility', 'justification' or 'just plain stupid' are close synonyms for cognitive dissonance, you're right. But, my friend, a rose by any other name is still an overpriced flower with thorns just waiting to prick your finger. Whatever you choose to call it, cognitive dissonance is always the unconscious reconciliation that often occurs when, in the face of undeniable facts, the mind is forced to hold contradictory beliefs. Since there is a direct link between gray matter and mouth, cognitive dissonance sufferers say and do some mighty stupid stuff. Reference the above examples.

Although international health organizations do not track the condition and no official records exist, one of the largest cognitive dissonance epidemics occurred in 1995. Like the influenza contagion of 1902 or a Madonna concert, it is a sad, sad thing to recall. Nearly one million poor schmucks in the United States and Europe were bitten by the bug. This is the amazing story of SoftRAM, a memory doubler for Windows 3.1 and Windows 95.

Say Buy Buy

Before getting to the juicy bits of our tale, some historical stage-setting is in order. You may remember way back in the early nineties when desktop technology was running amuck. Personal computers were selling twice as fast as proverbial hot-cakes. Fatter, hungrier software forced computer manufacturers to introduce new models every six weeks. 'Not Enough Memory' became more of a mantra than error message. Billion dollar 'fabs' (industry lingo for large, chip fabrication plants) popped up faster than fruit flies procreate, and still demand for PC memory outstripped supply by a wide margin. Memory prices checked in at around $25 per megabyte (NOTE: today the price of a megabyte is measured in pennies).

To make matters worse, Microsoft, cornered by Apple's slick user interface, was forced into the graphical user interface business. Windows 3.1 (the worst desktop operating system written by man or dog-boy) ate up about 3.5 meg. Its mutant cousin from Uranus, Windows 95, needed 8 megabytes of memory. And that, my friends, was only the tip of the iceberg. Both Windows operating systems used virtual memory—a fancy schmancy name for big swap files on dog-slow hard drives. If you didn't want to use virtual memory, 16MB was needed for 3.1 while the boys in Redmond recommended a whopping 32MB for Windows 95. Memory manufacturers thought they'd died, gone to heaven, and gotten a solid gold halo in the deal.

Poor users may have been bawling in their beer, but to software developers the global memory shortage dripped with opportunity. Their answer was quick, massive and cheap—the desktop memory manager. Companies like Quarterdeck introduced products using complex data compression algorithms. These products fiddled with Windows' memory scheme and squashed software into smaller chunks requiring less processing resources. The result (according to the advertisements) was dramatic increase in usable memory. These products were dubbed 'memory doublers.'

In 1995 an outfit called Syncronys Softcorp from Culver City, California introduced a memory doubler called SoftRAM. Here's the SoftRAM ad from the December 1995 issue of *Wired* Magazine.

"double click
"double memory

Doubling RAM doesn't have to be hard. Install SoftRAM95 and instantly speed up Windows 95 and Windows 3.0 and higher. Run multimedia and RAM hungry applications. Open more applications simultaneously. Say good-bye to 'Out of Memory' messages. 4MB becomes at least 8MB. 8MB becomes at least 16MB. Get the idea? (In fact, you can get up to 5 times more memory.) SoftRAM works with all 386 and higher desktops and laptops. PC Novice calls SoftRAM the 'real RAM doubler for Windows'.

Executive Summary: Don't Run Windows Without It. (TM)"

What a bargain!!! For a measly $35 you got a diskette and a ten-page instruction manual. Plop in the floppy, wait for the stuff to load, and immediately a jet-age control panel pops up complete with dials, counters, controls and everything. In 1995 this was very, very sexy. As the doubling proceeded, the needle on the left-hand gauge registered higher and higher as more RAM was created. Likewise, the dial on the right showed the percentage of free resources climbing. In the middle, rolling counters clicked away as physical RAM increased, virtual RAM decreased, and the total available memory freed up. When it was all over—abracadabra—RAM times two for less than fifty bucks.

Looking back in hindsight's rear view mirror, it is hard to say which was a bigger pile of hooey—the advertising hype or the sense of awe created by a sexy installation procedure. Didn't matter though. Two circumstances had converged to catapult SoftRAM's star into the stratosphere. Number 1—the trade press' constant whining about Windows' memory requirement scared the pants off the buying public. Number 2—SoftRAM signed an agreement with two large retailers to market Windows 95 and SoftRAM together.

Shoppers took to SoftRAM faster than mustard drips on your best shirt. Over 650,000 copies were gobbled up. The November 7, 1995 issue of *PC Magazine* reported SoftRAM was the top-selling piece of retail software in the US. Rainer Poetner, president of Syncronys, was named "Entrepreneur of the Year" by the Software Council of Southern California. Company stock jumped from three pennies a share in March 1995 to $32 a share by the next August. The *Wall Street Journal* asked, "Will it double your money, too?" In the fall, things got ugly.

Bad Memory

In the October 9, 1995 issue of *Business Week* (not exactly a beacon in the technical wilderness), Stephen Wildstrom wrote, "But both my casual tests and more formal benchmarking by National Software Testing Labs (like *Business Week,* a part of The McGraw-Hill Companies), found that the $35 SoftRAM 95 product had little effect on performance." The first real scientific nastiness about SoftRAM's technology showed up when Ingo Storm, a German software expert, and friends ran some benchmarks, decompiled the SoftRAM code, then published an expose in the October 12, 1995 issue of the German tech rag *Magazine fur Computer Technik*. Simply put, Storm and his buddies said the product didn't work worth a hoot. SoftRAM's German distributor promptly sued the author. By now, however, SoftRAM's sales had reached a cool $10 million. Behind the scenes the Federal Trade Commission had begun investigating SoftRAM. CEO's know this is never a good thing. The deal was sealed when *PC Magazine* completed a series of tests for an upcoming comparison of Windows memory utilities. Because of the brewing SoftRAM hubbub, the prestigious magazine chose to publish a rare 'special report.' The headline said it all: "SoftRAM95 Does Not Compress RAM in PC Magazine Test Labs" (http://www.zdnet.com/pcmag/special/reports/sr1107.htm). Microsoft served Syncronys with a "cease and desist" order forcing the little "Designed for Windows 95" tattoo to be removed from SoftRAM packing. Wow.

The Syncronys people sharpened their teeth and counterattacked. In a November 13th press release, the company president quoted a report from XXCAL labs saying "SoftRAM effectively doubles RAM." Other notable company quotes included "the compression code is well-hidden," and my personal favorite, "(evaluation) tools that have been used are 16-bit tools whereas Soft-RAM is made up of 32-bit code." As the evidence of SoftRam's masquerade became irrefutable, software 'bugs' were blamed (but not revealed). Despite the growing storm, DataQuest surveys showed most SoftRAM users were happy. Too late. The cat was out of the bag; the beans were spilt; the cookies had crumbled. All the spin in the world wouldn't change the fact that SoftRAM was, as Ingo Storm put it, nothing more than "Placebo Software."

No Guts

So what did the SoftRAM software do? The answer is a big, fat, "not much." If the intricacies of stone-age code float your boat, you can read Ingo Storm's painfully detailed report, "Placebo Plus" at www.heise.de/ct/english/95/12/100/. Certainly there are differences in the Windows 3.1 and 95 version of the product. Here's the Cliff Notes version of 'Inside SoftRAM95' published in the August 1996 edition of Dr. Dobbs's journal (if you want this report, it'll cost you $5 from Dr D's online archive). First, SoftRAM fragments conventional memory into chunks too small to be used by special software programs called DLLs. This provides more room for application code, and is a technique used in some form or fashion by most memory managers of the day. For Windows 3.1, SoftRAM changes the size of the Temporary Swap File beyond what was specified by the user. Of course, this only occurs if 'Permanent Swap File' is not used. Savvy Windows users most often choose the permanent file because this pre-allocates used disk space more efficiently and delivers more performance oomph. A Temporary Swap file, on the other hand, is allocated virtually, so will be spread in 'holes' all over the drive. Bottom line—the Virtual Swap File trick is impossible to measure and will rarely deliver any performance gains. In Windows95, SoftRAM uses a secondary page file along with the normal swap file to manage memory. Regardless of the method, neither Storm nor the Dr. Dobbs report found any evidence of data compression or memory doubling. Likewise, there was no performance improvement. Buyers did get a cool dashboard looking thingy with dials that moved.

In the end, Syncronys and SoftRAM got what they deserved, but not before a million copies of the product were sold. SoftRAM 95 was recalled in December 1995. As a condition of settlement with the FTC, the company offered full credits or refunds to customers. In July 1998, Syncronys's latest product, UpgradeAID 98, was announced. Two days later company execs and their lawyers showed up in a California bankruptcy court. Just goes to show—users have long memories.

Let's recap—somebody creates software that doesn't work, the marketing department takes over, a million people buy it and have very few complaints, some even swear the product works, company stock soars, the CEO gets an award.

The label on my oatmeal says, "Soluble fiber from oatmeal may reduce the risk of heart disease" so I eat a bowl every day. The gasoline I use is supposed to clean my engine. Any day now my love life is going to improve because I bought a bottle of designer aftershave (it worked for the guy in the magazine ad). Is it the truth? Or has that old cognitive dissonance demon bitten me right on the butt?

Computer Factoid

fac · toid   \fak' toid'\'   *n:*a single fact
or statistic variously regarded as being
trivial, useless, unsubstantiated, etc.

Incident at the WordPerfect Help Desk

Rumor has it that this is a true story from the WordPerfect help desk. The dialogue was transcribed from the call monitoring system and leaked by sympathetic employees. As the story goes, the help desk employee in this story was fired, however, he/she sued the WordPerfect organization for "termination without cause."

"Ridge Hall computer assistance; may I help you?"

"Yes, well, I'm having trouble with WordPerfect."

"What sort of trouble?"

"Well, I was just typing along, and all of a sudden the words went away."

"Went away?"

"They disappeared."

"Hmmm. So what does your screen look like now?"

"Nothing."

"Nothing?"

"It's a blank; it won't accept anything when I type."

"Are you still in WordPerfect, or did you get out?"

"How do I tell?"

"Can you see the C: prompt on the screen?"

"What's a sea-prompt?"

"Never mind, can you move your cursor around the screen?"

"There isn't any cursor: I told you, it won't accept anything I type."

"Does your monitor have a power indicator?"

"What's a monitor?"

"It's the thing with the screen on it that looks like a TV. Does it have a little light that tells you when it's on?"

"I don't know."

"Well, then look on the back of the monitor and find where the power cord goes into it. Can you see that?"

"Yes, I think so."

"Great. Follow the cord to the plug, and tell me if it's plugged into the wall."

"Yes, it is."

"When you were behind the monitor, did you notice that there were two cables plugged into the back of it, not just one?"

"No."

"Well, there are. I need you to look back there again and find the other cable."

"Okay, here it is."

"Follow it for me, and tell me if it's plugged securely into the back of your computer."

"I can't reach."

"Uh huh. Well, can you see if it is?"

"No."

"Even if you maybe put your knee on something and lean way over?"

"Oh, it's not because I don't have the right angle—it's because it's dark."

"Dark?"

"Yes—the office light is off, and the only light I have is coming in from the window."

"Well, turn on the office light then."

"I can't."

"No? Why not?"

"Because there's a power failure."

"A power...........a power failure? Aha, okay, we've got it licked now. Do you still have the boxes and manuals and packing stuff your computer came in?"

"Well, yes, I keep them in the closet."

"Good. Go get them, and unplug your system and pack it up just like it was when you got it. Then take it back to the store you bought it from."

"Really? Is it that bad?"

"Yes, I'm afraid it is."

"Well, all right then, I suppose. What do I tell them?"

"Tell them you're too <expletive deleted> stupid to own a computer."

COMPUTER FACTOID

> **fac · toid** \fak' toid'\'   *n:* a single fact
> or statistic variously regarded as being
> trivial, useless, unsubstantiated, etc.

The Zapatista Effect

With the Internet, war has become a whole new ball game. Consider the latest flare-up in the Middle East. Along with the predictable rock-chucking-then-shoot-large-caliber-weapons-into-a-crowd scenes, CNN reports Arab computer hackers continually launch attacks on Jewish and pro-Israeli Web sites all over the world. 'Hacktivism' is taking its place in the world of global conflict as a thousand-year-old war spills into cyberspace. We should not be surprised. The notion of NetWar was predicted back in 1993 by Rand think tankers John J. Arquilla and David F. Ronfeldt in their report, "Cyberwar is Coming" (http://www.rand.org/cgi-bin/Abstracts/ordi/getabbydoc.pl?doc=RP-223&hilite=1&qs=Cyberwar). It has been spreading ever since.

Traditional war, according to Arquilla and Rondfeldt, is fought by military organizations organized in strict hierarchies. Privates report to corporals, corporals report to sergeants, sergeants report to lieutenants, and so on up the military food chain. The information revolution will erode these hierarchies and redraw the boundaries of political and military influence. Info-armies will organize into flat, wide networks that bombard enemies with information and misinformation. Arquilla and Rondfeldt point to the thirteenth century Mongol hordes and the Vietcong in Vietnam as models of network-based military structures. Both the Mongols and Vietcong organized forces into fast-moving networks with absolute command of battlefield information. And, by the way, both armies whipped major military powers.

Arquilla and Rondfeldt say cyberwar will be fought according to information-related principles. A force will seek to disrupt or destroy the enemy's information and communication systems. At the same time, info-warriors will attempt to control the "balance of information and knowledge," by outflanking and surrounding an enemy, not only with traditional forces, but also with global support and allies. This means using information networks to gather resources and information, and to coordinate movement. The Zapatista Rebels in Chiapas, Mexico were the first.

A Small War in Mexico

At first, it seemed that the Zapatista Rebellion would be just another short-lived flare up in one of Mexico's most impoverished regions. Ragtag rebels carrying the banner of land reform and political representation seized two villages and went public with their demands. The global media machine rushed to the scene, and for a while the rebels were in the spotlight. Mexican authorities responded with superior firepower; outgunned rebels retreated to mountain hideouts. Grwoing weary of bad hotels and dirty water, reporters moved on to bigger and better killing grounds in Eastern Europe. The Mexican state-owned media channels began a national propaganda campaign downplaying the plight of the rebels. The Zapatista rebellion was fading away. Then the Internet took over.

Zapatista sympathizers embraced the cause, spreading the rebels' message from Web site to Web site until a global information network supporting the rebellion had been established. Each time the Mexican government released propaganda about the rebellion, the Zapatistas would respond. Rebel leaders would counter "official" government versions by issuing their own communiqués. Within hours the Zapatista message had been posted on Web sites around the world.

According to Zapatista mythology, this cyber tit for tat was carried out by Subcommandante Marcos. Marcos, the mysterious ski-masked voice of the movement, was as prolific as he was defiant. Legends painted Marcos sitting in the jungle with his laptop, posting Zapatista material via satellites to sympathetic Web sites. Not true. Marcos's communiqués were smuggled out by journalists and other friendlies. Notes were transcribed or scanned, then sent to Web sites all around the globe.

As time went on, the Internet became an even more important weapon for the rebels. Using email, Zapatista leaders coordinated material support for their cause. Worldwide meetings to plan strategy and outline ideology were held in cyberspace. At one point, the Internet was used to organize meetings and protests in places like Australia and Argentina. In the final analysis, the Zapatistas used the Internet to "surround" the Mexican government with a network of global support. Using this network meant the rebels could counter any claim made by their enemy, and muster and organize resources from around the globe. Dr.

Harry Cleaver from the University of Texas at Austin has dubbed this movement using the Internet to wage war as the Zapatista Effect.

Other conflicts have built on the Zapatista's success. In August 1998, the U.S. State Department reported the world's first terrorist cyberattack. A group calling itself Internet Black Tigers sent "suicide email bombings" to Sri Lankan embassies in an attempt to counter pro-Tamil rebel propaganda. That same year, Serbian hackers in Yugoslavia used a targeted denial of service attack and the Melissa virus to disrupt NATO email servers. 'Hacktivists' from Pakistan defaced over forty global Web sites in order to spread their pro-Kashmiri message. Last but not least, it looks like the Russkis hacked network print queues at the Space and Naval Systems Warfare Center sometime during the spring or summer of 1999. Individually, these incidents may seem insignificant, but according to one Washington official these cyberattacks are the "portent of worse things to come."

Cyberwar will bring other changes. Any day now this author expects to see a new GINet Joe show up on the shelves of the local Toys "R" Us™. The soldier doll will come with fatigues, a laptop, and a one-year subscription to the hacker mag '2600'.

COMPUTER FACTOID

fac · toid \fak' toid'\'   *n:* a single fact
or statistic variously regarded as being
trivial, useless, unsubstantiated, etc.

The Birth of Baby Cha

Its gender is disguised by a diaper and whatever it is, it never blinks. In most screen savers, the rubbery infant endlessly cha cha chas in place, with gyrating shoulders and flapping hands, and playing air guitar to an eerie a cappella version of the B.J. Thomas classic "Hooked on a Feeling" that sounds like a recording by Hitler Youth on downers. Sometimes the little cutie can be found riding a Harley, sporting a film noir fedora or chasing Godzilla. There have been sitcom cameos, starring roles, Blockbuster commercials, and even a hotsy-totsy photo exhibit in New York called the Pixilated Baby. He or she has even been seen on television's lawyer sitcom *Ally McBeal.* There's no denying it; Baby Cha, a.k.a. The Dancing Baby or the Oogachaka Baby, has become one of the most recognizable icons of the digital age. Proud parents are Michael Girard and wife Sysan Amkraut, however the little dickens has had a long line of guardians.

The Blessed Event

In the early nineties, Girard and Amkraut were teaching in Holland. In 1993 the couple moved to Palo Alto, and with partner John Chadwick started a computer animation company called Unreal Pictures Inc. The group's first project was to create software for animating any three-dimensional character with two legs. Girard's idea was to use a set of Arthur Murray footprints to map locomotion. The team's first real demo was a dancing human skeleton. According to Girard, "The Cha Cha motion and the basic arm movement—the way the hand flips over the head—go way back to this very first prototype." Later versions added more character to the motion. Animator Robert Lurye added shoulder wiggle and made the skeleton bend over and play guitar. The product was released in August 1996 as Character Studio, a plug-in for 3D Studio Max.

Character Studio would automatically adjust for different skeletal structures so the software could be applied to any digital figure that walked on two legs. In fact, the product was shipped with figures of an alien, a chimp, a harlequin, a woman (said to be a rendering of Demi Moore), a monster, and a baby. Lurye and the Unreal team finally mapped the Cha Cha choreography onto the baby. A demonstration called Baby Cha was shown by a company called Kinetix at a conference and had unexpected consequences. Culturally speaking, we have too much baggage about how we expect babies to move and act. Seeing a rubbery, wiggling, un-winking infant doing the Cha Cha is 3D was just too disturbing. Girard discarded the demo.

Animation guru Ron Lussier, then working at LucasArts in San Rafael, California, decided to experiment with Unreal's Character Studio and Girard's Cha Cha baby. Baby's movement ('deformation' in animator lingo) had already been set up by John Chadwick of Unreal. Lussier decided to spruce things up. He added shoulder bounce, retimed the hands, and worked on the light and surfacing. The finished product was shown to LucasArts techies in September or October of 1996. Friends immediately began asking Lussier to email them a copy of his demo, and the Baby Cha legend was born.

Baby Cha spread like wildfire through cyberspace (one Seattle aircraft company's Intranet became so bogged down, a voice mail message ordered employees to stop forwarding Baby Cha attachments to coworkers—the message admitted the baby was funny). Almost at once, Baby Cha began to change. Lussier's version of Baby Cha was silent—music came later. Today's most recognizable version has Baby Cha groovin' to Blue Swede's rendition of "Hooked". The words are the same, but the now famous "ougachooga" chant throbs in the background. Later renderings include rap, the Macarena, and Peter Gabriel's "Digging in the Dirt." Today you can find downloadable movies of Baby cart wheeling, getting drunk, and being blown to smithereens. I'm sad to say, there's even an animation of Baby Cha stepping in a pile of dog doo.

COMPUTER FACTOID

fac · toid \fak' toid'\' *n:*a single fact
or statistic variously regarded as being
trivial, useless, unsubstantiated, etc.

Kahn's Con

In 1980, French immigrant and mathematician Philippe Kahn set about creating a company he believed would dominate the IBM PC software market. Kahn's first product would be Turbo Pascal, a version of the popular programming language originally developed by Niklaus Wirth in the late sixties. Kahn's plan started with a dialect of Pascal written by Danish wunderkind Anders Heylsberg. The idea was to cram Heylsberg's Pascal with features offered only by professional class programming languages. And if this weren't enough, the final product would sell for around fifty bucks—a staggering $500 less than its nearest commercial-grade competitor.

Kahn rented two small rooms in Scotts Valley, California, hired a few programmers, and went to work. By 1983 Turbo Pascal for the IBM PC was finished, and Kahn was ready to launch Borland International. Unfortunately, he was broke.

What You See Is...

Kahn needed a large chunk of advertising space in *Byte Magazine*, the premier publication for programmers and techies in the United States. Real estate in *Byte* was expensive, with a full-page advertisement easily costing several thousand dollars. Kahn didn't have the money, and knew he couldn't get it. He did, however, have a plan.

For his scheme to succeed, Kahn required a façade of breathtaking ascendancy. Borland International had to look like a company with plenty of dough, and one poised on the precipice of a spectacular success. A perceptual metamorphosis was in order. Kahn recruited his friends and hired temporary workers. He then arranged a meeting with one of *Byte Magazine's* advertising peddlers. When the sucker arrived, Borland's new "workforce" had transformed the dingy two-room corporate office into a whirlwind of activity. Well-dressed "employees" shuffled paper hither and yon, while fake calls kept phones ringing off the hook. "Employees" openly discussed plans for their upcoming wealth. Borland reeked of success.

The unsuspecting mark was asked to sit. The sting was in play. Off to the side was a large sheet of paper on which Kahn had written the names of every major computing magazine published in the United States. An ugly line had been drawn through *Byte Magazine* signaling the publication had been dropped from Borland's marketing campaign. "Here was this chart the guy thought he wasn't supposed to see," Kahn said. "So I pushed it out of the way."

Kahn apologized. *Byte Magazine* simply wasn't the right vehicle. Wrong audience. Borland's media blitz was complete, and the marketing budget was spoken for. *Byte* was out. Sorry. Maybe next time.

According to Kahn, the ad salesman began to plead, "You've got to try." *Byte Magazine* simply couldn't miss the launch of a product that was obviously poised to take the world by storm. Think of the magazine's reputation (not to mention the salesman's commission). There had to be a way. Kahn hesitated. He could not stop a well-oiled marketing plan that was well underway (in fact, Borland had not purchased advertising from a single media source). On second thought, there may be a way.

Kahn worked out a buy-now-pay-later deal. *Byte* would run a single full-page, color advertisement for Turbo Pascal in the November 1983 edition. The bill could be paid after sales started rolling in. Kahn and company expected to make about $20,000 from Turbo's first release. As a result of the ad, sales of Turbo Pascal approached $150,000. Borland International and Philippe Kahn were on the map—at least for a little while.

Right and Wrong

Seven years later, writers Amar Bhide and Howard H. Stevenson explored issues of business ethics in their article "Why Be Honest if Honesty Doesn't Pay" (September-October 1990, *The Harvard Business Review*). An early interview with Kahn describing the *Byte* scam was included. Thanks to Kahn's Con and other case studies from the real world, Bhide and Stevenson came to the conclusion that Sunday school teachers had it wrong. Treachery can pay. According to their article, "There is no compelling economic reason to tell the truth or keep one's

word. Punishment for the treacherous in the real world is neither swift nor sure."
Philippe Kahn knew this was true way back in '83.

Kahn's Full Page Ad in *Byte Magazine*
from December 1983
(Image courtesy of *Byte Magazine*)

fac · toid \fak' toid'\'   *n*:a single fact
or statistic variously regarded as being
trivial, useless, unsubstantiated, etc.

PawSense—IgNobel Prize Winner

On an afternoon in early October, crowds gather outside the opulent Sanders Theater at Harvard University. Ten minutes after the doors open, the walnut-paneled galleries are filled, and it's standing room only for hundreds of scientists, students, and eccentrics. To an outsider, only a few of these people appear close to normal. Some are dressed in spotted bovine jammies. Others sport Cat-in-the-Hat floppy top hats and tie dyed tuxedos. They look down onto a lone podium standing off to the side on a small stage. Opposite the podium sits a group of distinguished, international Nobel Laureates who, depending on their mood, might be sporting fake Groucho Marx glasses with moustaches, or sipping a concoction brewed from coffee beans ingested and then excreted by a luak (the luak is an Indonesia bobcat). Technicians from National Public Radio are poised to begin a live broadcast while journalists from the nation's most prestigious publications jockey for position.

The crowd turns raucous. In the third balcony, a group of rival MIT math nerds unfurls a banner proclaiming the Hofstadter-esq notion, "If You Define a Subset Of A Given Set You Are In Fact Defining A New Subset Of The Same Set That Is Not Part Of The First Set." Voices from the floor chant, "Knuth is God. Knuth is God. Knuth is God." Someone throws a sea sponge saturated with green ketchup. Ignoring the commotion, a lanky man with bushy black hair steps to the microphone. A reverent silence fills the room. The ceremony is about to begin. The famous and not-so-famous anxiously await the announcement of the IgNobel Prize recipients. There will be ten and only ten winners.

Sponsored by the *Annals of Improbable Research* (www.improb.com), the Ig, as it is affectionately dubbed by those in the know, seeks to award "achievements that cannot or should not be reproduced." A look at past winners will give you an idea of the intellectual depth required to take one of these babies home. In 1994 Dr. James Nolan et al captured the Ig for Medicine after publishing "The Acute Management of the Zipper Entrapped Penis" in *the Journal of Emergency Medicine*. That same year the IG for Entomology went to Dr. Mark Hostetler for his pioneering work, "The Gunk on Your Car," a guide for identifying insect splats on your windshield. On the international front, Takeshi Makino, president of a Japanese detective agency, received the 1999 Chemistry Ig for his involvement with S-Check, a spray that wives apply to their husbands' underwear to detect infidelity.

Computer Science Gets the Ig

Although the list of Ig recipients is impressive, notables from the field of Computer Science have been conspicuously absent from the winner's circle. Admittedly, several past winners have used computers in their work. The Southern Baptist Church of Alabama (Ig for Mathematics, 1994), for example, used computers to estimate how many Alabama citizens would go to Hell if they didn't repent. Jan Pablo Davila (Ig for Economics, 1994), a financial futures trader for Chile, lost an amount equal to .5% of his country's GNP when he mistakenly instructed his laptop computer to "buy" when he meant "sell." In addition to being awarded the Ig, Davila's booboo spawned a new verb in Chile. To 'davilar' means to royally screw things up. Despite these milestones, there was never an IgNobel recognizing achievements in the field of computer science—never, that is, until 2000.

In 2000, the IgNobel Prize in Computer Science was awarded to Mr. Chris Niswander, a programmer from Tucson, Arizona, for developing software that detects a cat walking across your computer keyboard. His product is called PawSense.

To this writer's thinking, one should never own a pet that is too big to flush down the toilet when vacation time rolls around. Writing pet-targeted software seems a bit much. Pet owners typically disagree, and for cat owners especially, the value of Niswander's work is obvious. Everyone knows kitty cats eat what they want, sleep where they want, poop where they want, and walk where they want. In fact, it is easier to control sailors in a border town on a Saturday night than the family cat. Coughed-up hairballs on dinner plates notwithstanding, real problems can occur if Tabby decides to stroll across your computer keyboard. With today's shortcut keys and control codes, funky keystroke combinations caused by kitty paws can damage data, delete files, create unexpected configuration changes, and even crash the computer. PawSense uses groundbreaking research and innovative engineering to solve this problem.

A few sourpusses (no pun intended) on the IgNobel Awards Council speculated that PawSense is a rip-off of "Kitten on the Keys", a ragtime piece for piano written in 1921 by Zez Comfry. "No way," says Niswander. In an interview with *Cyberwalker*, the young programmer claims the light came on when a cat named Deimos "crashed his sister's computer and uninstalled some software." Whatever the inspiration, Niswander began studying the mechanics and geometry of the kitty paw. He superimposed shapes of cat tootsies onto dozens of computer keyboards, and analyzed "paw angles and toe positions." Hours of painstaking analysis revealed all possible feline keystroke combinations. Niswander then wrote software that detected computer keystrokes created by kitty cat feet. But this was only half the battle.

CAT-LIKE TYPING DETECTED

To protect other programs, PawSense is diverting keyboard input.
Click the button below to close this window.

> Let me use the computer!

> Change Settings

You can also exit this window by typing the word "human".

`ffffgfg`

If you want to terminate PawSense, type "terminate".

Warning Screen from PawSense
(Image courtesy of Chris Niswander)

Niswander had to devise a way to get the pesky pet off the keyboard. During alpha tests with a subject named Roo, Niswander experimented with sounds cats would find offensive. He settled on a wheezing harmonica sounding as if it is stuck in someone's windpipe. Once a kitty is caught keyboard walking, PawSense disables the computer keyboard, displays the message "CAT-LIKE TYPING DETECTED", and begins playing the Gasping Harmonica Concerto (PawSense also comes with a loud hissing noise). Other sounds can be recorded and configured by the user. Packaged as a Terminate-Stay-Resident (TSR) program, PawSense can be automatically loaded each time the computer is booted.

List price for PawSense is $19.99 plus shipping and handling, and can be purchased at www.bitboost.com/pawsense/index.html. The product comes with a printed user's manual and a robust array of configuration options including "Pick Annoying Sound" and a sensitivity setting. Versions are available for Windows 95/98, NT and 2000. Sorry, the Mac version is still "in development."

As with all great minds, Niswander won't be caught resting on his laurels. He is currently developing a product called BabySense. Personally, I'd like to see Niswander find another niche. I'll really start to worry if I see a product called ButtSense hit the market.

Computer Factoid

fac · toid \fak' toid'\`   *n:* a single fact
or statistic variously regarded as being
trivial, useless, unsubstantiated, etc.

Cabbage Divine

Apparitions of the Virgin Mary are nothing new. The devout have seen her visage in the cloudless sky above the Mojave Desert, burned on the wall of a church in Sri Lanka in a flash of light, and woven in an "ayate" or cloak of a Mexican peasant. When it happens, word spreads like wildfire, and zealots make pilgrimages to the sightings offering prayers and asking for divine intervention. We all knew it was just a matter of time. Now the Virgin Mary has been spotted on the Internet—in a plate of pickled cabbage on the Web site of a Korean restaurant.

Prank, you're thinking? Urban legend? Just plain stupid? Could be. But this writer has traveled all around this big old world a time or two and, yessirree Bob, I've seen some mighty bizarre things. So my friend, you'll have to make up your own mind on this one.

According to the tale, San Francisco native Janet Liu was waiting for her daughter at a friend's house. It was just about suppertime and Liu's friend was ordering take-out from a local Korean restaurant. The Web page of Family's Korean Bar B Que #2 was on the screen. There were a picture of the restaurant, a map, and descriptions of the daily specials. Then something inexplicable caught Liu's eye. The screen hypnotized her. Ms Liu found herself staring at a digitized image of the house specialty—a big, ole, yummy plate of white kimchi or Korean pickled cabbage. No doubt about it (at least in the mind of the beholder)—smack dab in the middle of the swirling yellowish goo was an image of the Blessed Virgin Mary. Somebody went nuts and called the local Cantonese radio station, KVTO.

Kimchi and the Virgin Mary
(Image courtesy of Korean Family Bar B Que #2)

"I had an uncontrollable desire to cry, so I cried," Liu told a KVTO interviewer. "I called my daughter over and told her to look at the screen and asked her if she saw the Virgin Mary and she did."

An hour after the Liu interview was aired, Chung Rae Lee, owner of Family's Korean BBQ #2 and a practicing Presbyterian, became overwhelmed with telephone calls from persons claiming to have seen the Blessed Virgin. Believing the sightings would be bad for business, Mr. Rae Lee removed the plate-of-cabbage image, but community pressure was too much, and within a few hours, the kimchi graphic was back on the Web. "I do not want to hide this image," Mr. Rae Lee said. "But this is not a business advertisement. We want only to respect an image that is important to so many people. If they want to visit that is OK with us, too."

As of May 1999, the Family's Korean BBQ#2 Web site had reportedly been visited over 40,000 times by the curious as well as the devout. Mr. Rae Lee has received gifts and flowers, not to mention tons of email, thanking him for maintaining the image of the Holy Mother.

Don't believe me? Visit http://www.geocities.com/Tokyo/Bridge/7601/and form your own opinion. But let me warn you. The Family's Korean BBQ#2 Web page is only for the devout. The site counter is gone and the email address is no longer active. If you find that Mr. Rae Lee's plate of cabbage doesn't look like the Blessed Virgin, don't call me.

COMPUTER FACTOID

fac · toid \fak' toid"\' _n:_ a single fact
or statistic variously regarded as being
trivial, useless, unsubstantiated, etc.

Pathological Internet Use

QUESTION: What's the difference between a bad habit and a vice?
ANSWER: A vice has its own official behavior disorder.

In August 1997 cyberspace attained the same profligacy as gambling, drugs, alcohol, and too many Reese's Peanut Butter Cups when the American Psychological Association recognized Pathological Internet Use (or PIU) as a legitimate behavior disorder. The event took place after Dr. Kimberly Young, a psychologist from the University of Pittsburgh at Bradford, presented groundbreaking work at the 105th Annual Convention of the American Psychological Association in Chicago. According to Dr. Young's findings, the Internet is indeed addictive.

Dr. Young used Web-based surveys to study the online habits of 396 dispersed World Wide Web users. Results showed about 90% of the respondents became addicted to the "two-way communication functions: chat rooms, MUDS (multi-user dungeons) newsgroups and email." Internet surfing and information-related tools (gophers, FTP sites) do not seem to lead to high levels of dependency (only about 9% of study respondents were addicted to downloads—go figure). According to Dr. Young, the average Internet junkie spends about thirty-eight hours per week online, dealing with non-employment/non-academic matters compared with only eight hours for non-addicts. PIU sufferers reported getting less than four hours of sleep per night due to after-hours Internet soirees. Although the cause and effect pathology is not known, heavy PIU victims are more likely to suffer from significant depression. Many have a history of depressive disorders.

Internetomania

A 1998 study of "Internetomania" carried out by Dr. Nathan Shapira of the University of Cincinnati seems to confirm Young's results. According to Dr. Shapira "Internetomaniacs" (his term, not mine) feel a rush as soon as they log on. "They get a real burst of energy, their mood perks up; it's quite a thrill." An Internet high can last four of five hours and even continue after the subject has signed off. Yet the effects of "Internetomania" can be devastating. Nathan cites cases of chronic unemployment and crumbling romantic relationships. In one case a college student became so hooked he stopped going to class and could not be reached by his parents. By the time he was found he had logged over two hundred fifty continuous Internet hours and racked up online charges for $400.

The demographics of Shapira's subjects looked a lot like those found in Dr. Young's study. Both Shapira and Young found an equal split between men and women. For Shapira's Internetomaniacs, time on the Internet averaged from thirty to thirty-five hours per week (also similar to Young's findings). This was in addition to time spent on computers at work. Most subjects had at least a bachelor's degree.

The anonymity of the Internet, according to the experts, is the main attraction for potential addicts. People enjoy creating a new persona and acting in ways they never would in real life. One survey participant admitted, "By day, I am a mild-mannered husband, but at night I become an aggressive bastard online." Some addicts create online identities to compensate for low esteem or feelings of inadequacy. Others use the Internet as a distraction for other problems in their lives. Some even use chat rooms and news groups to create and test personalities before trying them out in the real world.

Once a person is hooked, their uncontrolled Internet use can establish a predictable cycle of mood swings, lack of sleep, fatigue, poor eating habits, and personal isolation. These are they very same habits leading to intense treatment with chemicals like Lithium or other mood stabilizing drugs. So, this writer wants to know—what's the problem? We'd all just be watching TV or going bowling anyway.

Not Me

OK—time for a little honesty. Does all this talk about PIU make you nervous? Do you get the shakes after a couple of hours away from your laptop? Are you starting to have your chat room handle printed on your business cards?

Have you heard your family whispering about your deteriorating personal hygiene? You could be hooked and not even know it.

Here's an abbreviated form of Dr. Young's survey for determining Pathological Internet Use. Go ahead. It's just for fun.

Do you:

1. feel preoccupied with the Internet? (i.e. thinking about the Internet when offline).

2. feel a need to use the Internet with increasing amounts of time in order to achieve satisfaction?

3. have an inability to control your Internet use?

4. feel restless or irritable when attempting to cut down or stop Internet use?

5. use the Internet as a way of escaping from problems or of relieving a poor mood (i.e., feelings of helplessness, guilt, anxiety, or depression)?

6. lie to family members or friends to conceal the extent of involvement with the Internet?

7. jeopardize or risk the loss of significant relationship, job, educational or career opportunity because of the Internet?

8. after spending an excessive amount of money on online fees, often return another day?

9. go through withdrawal when offline (e.g., increased depression, anxiety, etc.)?

10. stay online longer than originally attended?

Individuals who met four or more of these criteria during a 12-month period were classified as dependent.

Source: the University of Pittsburgh at Bradford.

Help is on the Way

If you think the old Internet monkey is on your back, trust me. Help is on the way. Plenty of practicing psychologists today treat PIU, and support groups for the disorder are popping up everywhere. Harvard's got an Internet Addiction program. So does the University of Massachusetts. Then again, if you're shy or simply can't tear yourself away from your keyboard, you could visit Dr. Young's online addiction clinic at www.netaddiction.com. You'll find lots of information resources about PIU and addictive Internet use. Hardcore I-junkies can subscribe to Dr. Young's Online Chat Room Counseling. At this writing, a little virtual therapy can be arranged in fifty-minute intervals for $89 each, or purchased through the Multiple Counseling Package Plan of three chat room sessions for an introductory rate of $239. Dr. Young also provides treatment via email. The One Session deal includes an extensive email reply for the one-time fee of $25.00. Sign up for the Multiple Session Plan and you'll receive three ongoing emails for the introductory rate of $60. Credit cards are accepted. Billing is discreet.

Email Sessions. Counseling in chat rooms. Call me bewildered, call me puzzled, call me confused, but treating PIU online sounds lot like holding an Alcoholics Anonymous meeting and serving martinis at the break.

COMPUTER FACTOID

fac · toid \fak' toid'\ *n*:a single fact
or statistic variously regarded as being
trivial, useless, unsubstantiated, etc.

Buddy, Can You Spare a Dime?
(PayPal Accepted)

Really smart people keep saying the Internet has changed the way we live. For years I was not convinced. Yeah, I know, a guy can put on lipstick, get dressed up in his wife's underwear, and buy a book from Amazon.com all in the privacy of his own home. Big deal. Anyway, the other day I had a cyberspace epiphany. My skepticism was swept away, and I was convinced once and for all. The Internet has changed our lives. Here's what happened.

Every day I drive to my luxuriously appointed cubicle in a large southwestern city. My drive to work takes me through a dozen intersections. Every time I stop at a red light or stop sign one or more panhandlers approaches me. You know—these guys on street corners, looking pitiful and holding up signs ending in "God Bless" handwritten on pieces of cardboard. A few years ago things weren't so bad, but now these people are thicker than the hairs sticking out of my Aunt Ethel's ears.

Don't get me wrong. I feel badly for these people. Really. I'd like to give them some spare change, or even a can or two of creamed asparagus, but rolling down my window gives me the willies. They look kind of dirty, and their oral hygiene habits aren't so good either. Every day I have crises of consciousness, so to speak, while driving to work. By the time I get to the office, I'm a guilt-ridden mass of quivering jelly. The Internet changed all this when a friend suggested I check out panhandling online.

At first I didn't believe her, but it's true. Now you can help the down-and-out without leaving the comfort of your dial-up connection. Think of it. Going out for that six-pack means never having to say you're sorry. It's as easy as PayPal. So, as a service to the psychological health of our readers, let me proudly present my Top Ten Online Panhandling Sites. Get your hankies and spare change ready.

Save Karyn

http://www.savekaryn.com/

Here's the site that started it all. Karyn did a bad thing. This N.Y. gal got herself between a rock and a hard place by racking up twenty grand in credit card debt using King Visa to buy too many early morning lattes and $100 shoes on eBay™. Personally, I think this explanation is a bit dodgy, but this girl's got cajones bigger than bowling balls. Her ramblings plead for people to send her a buck. If you believe her Web site, it worked. She's out of debt. As of November 2002 she claims to have received over $13K (she raised the rest by selling her stuff on eBay). To be honest, I didn't send Karyn a dollar, because the way I figure it for that much money I ought to see some naked pictures. If you check the site today you'll learn that Karyn doesn't need help anymore. Debt-free and with a couple of books on eBay, looks like Karyn hit online pay dirt. Only in America.

123Save Me

http://www.123saveme.com/

Meet Lisa. She's in worse shape than Karyn. The Wicked Credit Card Witch of the West has got her pegged for a $30,000 bill. Lisa is serious about getting out of debt because her Web site says so. There's even a picture of Lisa cutting up her credit card. Features of the site include a "Letter from Lisa," "Grand Debt Tally," a "Lisa Thanks You" message, and a link to PayPal.

Street Beggin'

http://www.geocities.com/Heartland/Bluffs/8105/index.html

I love honesty. On this site, Ricky of Fort Wayne, Indiana admits he's "homeless, half-drunk, unemployed, dumb as a rock, and broke." There's a picture of Ricky panhandling on the street, but rising vice prices are forcing him to reach out into cyberspace. A six-pack of Natural Light costs $2.99, while generic smokes are running $1.89. What's a guy to do? If this doesn't choke you up, check out Ricky's link to the story of his girlfriend. She's a homeless deaf mute named Pinky. If things weren't bad enough, Pinky has been kidnapped and the dirty so-and-so's are demanding $50,000 in unmarked bills.

Save Elaine

http://www.saveelaine.com/

Want to know why you shouldn't get a bachelor's degree in music? Try a $40,000 student loan bill and no J—O—B. Student loans aside, Elaine wants to be an opera singer and wants to sign up for some very expensive voice lessons. She needs help. Click on her Web site to hear her sing. Besides being up to her larynx in debt, the old biological clock is counting down. Elaine is twenty-nine and the female voice reaches maturity at thirty-five. She needs to start those lessons soon. "Hurry," Elaine says.

Help Me Save My Hair

http://www.shinynoggin.com/

Kent lives in St. Louis, has two dogs, and is financially responsible. Trouble is, Kent is going bald. Judging from the picture on his Web site, in less than a year the dome of Kent's noodle will be shinier than a buffed light bulb. He's got a Baldy Blog chronicling every failing follicle. I've got to give the guy credit. He's exploring every angle. He's got a link to a comb-over site in the U.K. (www.combovers.co.uk). Kent's got a good heart. Send him money for his hair transplant and you get to help pick his community service action for the week.

Help a Girl Fill Out Her Sweater

http://www.giveboobs.com/

This is my kind of panhandling. "Help a girl fill out a sweater," says Michel's (pronounced Michelle) Web site. My pleasure, I say. To tell you the truth, Michel looks fine to me with her 34As, but what do I know? She's pandering Netizens for a $4,500 boob job and needs our help. Judging by her "Boob Fund Progress" page (this is where visitors can keep a-breast of the situation), Michel is doing something right. Since November 2002, she's raised over $3,400. With this kind of money at stake, Michel's got me thinking about a boob job.

Mr. Biff's Toejam

http://home.att.net/~mr.biff/wsb/html/view.cgi-home.html-.html

Hold on to your pocket protector. Click on this link and the first thing you see is a naked old guy sitting in front of a computer, his arm strategically blocking the shriveled parts. The text says Mr. Biff has lost his shirt and he wants you to send him a dollar. That's about all I can tell you about this one.

Help Dick Mac Live

http://www.geocities.com/dickmac999/index.html

It's expensive to live in New York City. Dick Mac should know. He lives a Manhattan lifestyle but is having some trouble making ends meet. He'd like a bunch of total strangers, including you and me, to help. Poor Dick. He's got some pretty heavy expenses coming up. He posts these on his Web site. He wants his wife to throw him a birthday bash for $1,000. In March he needs another five grand for a Las Vegas trip. Dick's art collection needs updating too. Life sure can be tough sometimes.

Help a Family in Need

http://www.expage.com/page/helpafamilyinneed

A real tearjerker. According to this site, Don is a Gulf War vet who got downsized. Car's busted. Wife's out of work. Lots of medical bills. The food banks don't carry fresh fruits. No pictures, address, or last name, doggone it.

Send Me a Dollar

http://www.sendmeadollar.com

I wouldn't advise giving this guy any money. He just asks that you open your wallet and send him a buck for no reason that I can see. I would, however, recommend his site. His "Rate-A-Begger" links list over one hundred fifty online panhandling Web sites. If you can't find something here that pulls on your heartstrings, then pal, you ain't got no heart.

Begging online. Thanks to the Internet my shame is gone. An hour or two of surfing the Cyber panhandlers and I feel like a new man, my selfishness absolved. Each day I look forward the drive to work when I can stop at a red light, keep my hands on the wheel, and stare straight ahead. No guilt. No remorse. And the best part—I get to keep my can of creamed asparagus.

COMPUTER FACTOID

fac · toid \fak' toid'\'   _n:_a single fact
or statistic variously regarded as being
trivial, useless, unsubstantiated, etc.

Symphony for Dot Matrix Printers

Sometimes the musical metaphor is as clear as the nose on your face. There's Mozart's dead daddy resurrected in the opera *Don Giovanni*, or Peter, Paul and Mary's not-so-veiled reference to wacky tabacky in "Puff the Magic Dragon." If musical interpretation is your strong suit, try this on for size. Two Canadians Thomas McIntosh and Emmanuel Madan have composed a thirty-five-minute symphony performed entirely by obsolete dot matrix printers. What could it all mean, you ask?

Madan and McIntosh, who call themselves "The User" like to say they "inhabit the trailing edge of technology." "This vantage point," they pontificate, "affords an excellent view of technology from behind." The "technology from behind" imagery may make sense to you, but this writer has visions of being mooned by an IBM 360. Official symphony press releases and interviews are chock-full of this kind of heady stuff.

Here are a couple of examples from the Italian magazine *Neural.*

"People are slaves, in that they have no choice but to go to the office every day. They're completely in debt...they're slaves."

So, what's new?

"de Certeau suggests that each and every one of us take a little of our employer's time and resources to produce something unnecessary—to practice a minute but universal form of subversive creativity."

de Certeau. Isn't he the guy who invented breath mints with Retsin?

Being a lowly tech writer who proudly shops at Target, I decided to bypass the intellectual mumbo jumbo and get to the bottom of things myself. After some serious phone tag, I finally contacted McIntosh in his Quebec City office. I am happy to report he's an intelligent, pleasant, young-sounding guy who didn't use a lot of big words, and said things I could understand.

Two Men and a Printer

An architect by training, McIntosh told me he was working in a structure when he noticed being surrounded by exceptional acoustics. He knew he had to do something with sound, and called his amigo Madan, a musician and composer. Their first collaboration was the silophone—an attempt to turn an abandoned grain silo into one very large concrete flute. Money problems forced our heroes to seek another direction, and the two settled on old dot matrix printers as sources of sound. After some serious scrounging and a little free moolah from *Le Conseil des Arts et des Lettres de Quebec*, their dot matrix orchestra was born. Original band members include a Juki, Epson TX-80B, a Star Micronic Gemini 10X, and more. At this writing, the guys are looking for an Apple Style Writer, an Epson TX-80B "Essna," and a Citizen Swift. Contact theuser@sat.qc.ca if you've got one of these things lying around.

Even though all art is derivative, you may be surprised to learn that *The Symphony for Dot Matrix Printers* is not the first time printers have been used to make music. I have personally wasted untold hours and reams of my ex-employer's green-bar paper while programming calypso rhythms on a pair of large DEC line printers. The musical capabilities of early IBM printers are well known. Way back in 1963, programmers noticed that diagnostic routines created a "frequency buzz" on the Model 701. Oscilloscopes in hand, sly prop-heads discovered certain instructions produced identifiable tones. It didn't take long before every airhead on the night shift was creating music. "Three Blind Mice" is reportedly the first tune transcribed for a computer printer. Christmas carols soon became popular. IBM printer music reached its zenith with the IBM 1403. The 1403 used a spinning print chain and hammers capable of spewing out 1400 132-column lines per minute. That's less than three seconds per page, and that's a lot of noise. There are still a few 1403 recordings hanging around the Internet including toe tappers like "She'll Be Comin' Round the Mountain" and "Ode to Joy."

McIntosh was unaware of the 1403 legacy but did know about the Dutch musician Paul Panhuysen. On his CD, "Engines in Power and Love" (Het Apollohuis), Panhuysen uses dot matrix printers to produce a droning background noise. McIntosh and Madan take a completely different approach. Their symphony is the first work of its kind to be performed entirely by printers. The composition is mind-boggling, but admittedly difficult to dance to.

Sound Printing

Every printer must be auditioned. "We need to know what kind of noise each machine can produce," says McIntosh. "Put the noises together and we can make a symphony." Noises coming out of a particular brand of dot matrix printer are completely unique. For example, the motor in the Epson LQ 1050 is always running, producing a low, pleasant hum like the constant strumming of a chord. The fast print-head action of the Citizen Swift is used for bursts of staccato and rapid sections of the symphony. Once the orchestra is assembled and tuned, the score must be composed. Here's where the work really begins.

Two strategies are employed for composing dot matrix music. First, the unique sonority of each printer is identified. Then a printed page for rhythm and tone is laid out and programmed. The computer program controlling the thirty-five-minute symphony is about one hundred pages of ASCII characters. If you think all this sounds easy, think again. McIntosh estimates that one minute of dot matrix printer music requires two weeks of design and programming. Once the score is complete, it is loaded onto a network server attached to the printers. Up until now, the symphony server has driven twelve printers simultaneously. For an upcoming concert in Germany, the McIntosh and Madan will use a total of fourteen dot matrix musicians.

On the Road Again

"When it comes to the music, surprise is on our side. People come expecting something flaky and are surprised by the complexity of the sounds they hear."

The Dot Matrix Symphony in Barcelona
(Image courtesy of The User)

Judging from the symphony's performance schedule, lots of people have been surprised. *The Symphony for Dot Matrix Printers* has been performed around Canada, the United States, and Europe. At the Wood Street Gallery in Pittsburgh, Pennsylvania, an office environment was set up complete with desks, walls, chairs, and lamps. Printers were scattered around just like in a real big-business sweatshop. Patrons were invited to sit at "their desks" while the symphony was being performed in hopes the chatter would produce a horrifying "deja vu." In Barcelona, the symphony was performed on a traditional stage. Other venues will be explored and exposed as McIntosh and Madan begin a European tour later this year.

And just in case you're wondering—yes, there is a CD of *The Symphony for Dot Matrix Printers* produced by Staalplaat in Amsterdam and distributed by Soleilmoon in Portland. There's a copy in my CD rack as we speak.

I admit it. When I first heard about *The Symphony for Dot Matrix Printers* I thought—"how screwy can you get?" I did a little research. I talked to people, interviewed McIntosh, and heard the work for myself. Here's the bottom line. No matter what we may think, Thomas McIntosh and Emmanuel Madan are doing incredibly creative work (don't forget—Mozart died penniless and forgotten). They're cutting CDs and have toured Europe. They probably don't have to tuck in their shirttails when they go to work, or sit in a cubicle all day. Me—I commute down the freeway at 6:00 A.M. strangled by a useless necktie then sit behind the same desk all day, day after day. If things go well this summer, I'll probably drive to Cleveland for some R & R at the Day's Inn. By the way, how's your life going?

COMPUTER FACTOID

fac · toid \fak' toid'\'   *n*:a single fact
or statistic variously regarded as being
trivial, useless, unsubstantiated, etc.

GOG: The First Cyber Villain

What was the first computer cast as a villain in a movie? The most common answers are the Hal the psychotic computer from *2001: A Space Odyssey* (1968) or Yul Brynner's cyber cowboy in *Westworld* (1973). Both answers are wrong.

The First Digital Malefactor in a Movie Award goes to *GOG: Frankenstein of Steel,* from a 1954 sci-fi B flick directed by Herbert "Blood-of-Dracula" Strock. Ivan Tors wrote the script (probably between lunch and happy hour) at the height of the Cold War paranoia. Like all 1950s sci-fi flicks, GOG has the three mandatory elements of plot; 1) Commies, 2) radiation, and 3) a hero who gets the girl but never kisses her on screen. You can't find GOG at your local video store or at Amazon.com. My copy came from eBay and looks like a dupe from a TV broadcast somewhere in the Far East. The story line goes something like this.

The United States is building a space station in a ultra-secret, underground facility in New Mexico. Unfortunately, top scientists on the project keep getting bumped off when laboratory gizmos mysteriously go haywire. One guy gets strangled by a pair of robotic arms. A little later a husband and wife team find themselves on the wrong side of a locked sub-zero freezer door and they get turned into a pair of popsicles. Head honcho scientist Dr. Van Ness (Herbert Marshall) becomes suspicious and asks Washington for help. Office of Scientific Investigations (OSI) operative Dr. David Sheppard (Richard Eagan) flies to New Mexico in a remote-controlled helicopter (the center is supposed to be a secret, so a pilot wouldn't do).

The first thing Dr. Sheppard does after landing is change into coveralls and penny loafers. In a briefing with center officials, Sheppard makes eye contact with blond bombshell Joanna Merritt (Constance Dowling) who is also dressed in coveralls and penny loafers. (NOTE: Dowling was writer Tor's real-life wife). You can tell by those "looks" that there's more to Sheppard and Merritt than meets the eye. The love interest is in play. Merritt is really a 'plant' from the OSI, so she and Dr. Sheppard secretly team up on the investigation. You can tell they want to kiss but never do because they have important work to do. Meanwhile, more scientists get deep-sixed.

The Plot Thickens

A lot of the center's grunt work is done by GOG and MAGOG, two robots who look remarkably like my mom's Hoover upright, only with arms. After some sniffing around, Sheppard notices that GOG and MAGOG have been suspiciously close to a couple of the "accidents." He also learns that everything in the labs, including GOG and MAGOG, is controlled by something called a Nuclear Operated Variable Automatic Computer, or NOVAC.

Little does Sheppard know, those pesky robots were manufactured in a friendly Eastern European country. Before being shipped to the U.S. of A., enemy agents slipped a radio transmitter into GOG's innards. Eastern European evildoers are using GOG's transmitter to reprogram NOVAC. The supercomputer is murdering scientists, thus sabotaging the free world's space defense program. Those filthy so-and-so's.

One side note: Sheppard should have been suspicious from the beginning, since the names GOG and MAGOG refer to evil beings whom Satan will use to usher in the end of the world (Revelation 20). So much for obvious clues.

When Dr. S. finally figures things out, he goes after GOG. NOVAC knows Sheppard knows. Sheppard knows Novac knows Sheppard knows. Our man from the OSI has got to get that transmitter. Ominous music. Chase scene. GOG flips a switch and lays down a deadly dose of radiation, but to no avail. Our hero is protected by his tinfoil suit. His girlfriend isn't wearing her tinfoil suit so she passes out. The denouement is reached when Dr. Sheppard barbecues GOG with a flamethrower. All is well. NOVAC can be reprogrammed to do good. Democracy is saved.

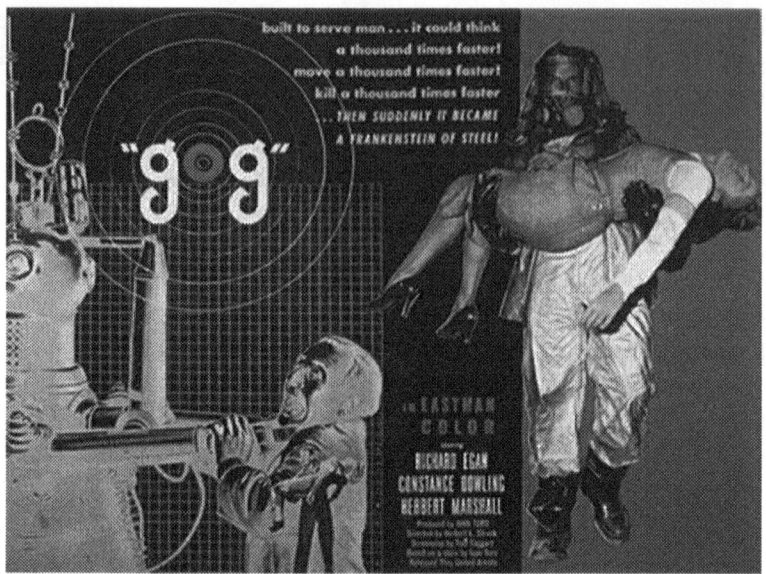

1954 GOG Lobby Card
(From the author's factoid collection)

Tors may not have been a sci-fi prophet. In fact, he may have written GOG just to get his ex-chorus-girl wife a movie part. Still, the movie does have some uncanny predictions. There's the wireless method NOVAC uses to control GOG and the laboratories. Stealth technology appears when scientists discover a high-flying enemy aircraft made of non-metallic materials, thus making it invisible to radar. On the other hand, Tors's story has a fair number of misses. NOVAC is a supercomputer programmed with punched paper tape. Then there's all this radiation. At the end of the movie Dr. Sheppard leans over a bedridden Joanna, who's recovering from a mega slam of radioactivity. "Don't worry," he says. "You'll be fine in a couple of days."

fac · toid   \fak' toid"\'   *n*:a single fact
or statistic variously regarded as being
trivial, useless, unsubstantiated, etc.

E Divorce

or

Honey, Don't Forget Your Cell Phone

Islam. Now here's a religion that's got the mechanics of this divorce business down pat. According to strict Sharia Law, if a Muslim husband wants to get unhitched, all he's got to do is proclaim loudly and clearly, "I divorce you" three times to his wife and voilà—the matrimonial union is dissolved.

To be recognized as a legitimate divorce, an Islamic court must be able to verify that the guy really meant it, and the gal received the divorce pronouncement. For the past couple of hundred years, this meant husbands had to round up a few of their pals and bring them along to witness the pronouncing. Coming from a religion that won't let a guy have a ham sandwich and a beer during the game, this faster-than-a-Las-Vegas-divorce sounds a tad paradoxical. With satellite communications and SMS (Short Messaging Service or text messaging), Islamic divorce has entered the digital age.

In Dubai, a tiny but filthy rich Arab Emirate off the coast of Saudi Arabia, the June 2001 issue of the *Gulf News* reported that a man divorced his wife using the text-messaging feature of her cell phone. According to the story, the woman missed her curfew and received the message, "Why are you late? You are divorced." from her impatient hubby. Isolated incident, you ask? A hoax, perhaps? Too good to be true, you're thinking? Nope. Investigative reporters at the *Gulf News* turned up a total of sixteen cases of text-messaging divorce in Dubai between April and June of 2001. The Dubai-ians aren't alone. Word spread, and before long Muslim husbands everywhere were whipping out their cell phones and dialing D for Get-The-Heck-Out-of-My-Life. Just goes to show, you can't stand in the way of an idea whose time has come.

Who Said?

As one would expect, the first E-Divorce in Dubai caused quite a stir. One Abdel-Salem Darwish, a counselor in the Family Reconciliation section of the country's courts, told a *News* reporter that his department ran the cell-phone divorce question up the flagpole with other Islamic higher-ups. Scholars in Dubai Awqaf and Islamic Affairs Department, the Arabic and Islamic College in Dubai, and other religious experts in Saudi Arabia all said the same thing. "The divorce is valid, as long as the husband expressed the will to divorce and the wife received it."

As the text-messaging divorce phenomenon spread to places like Pakistan, Qatar, and Kuala Lumpur, religious higher-ups all had something to say. The Mufti (not to be confused with a furry hand warmer or dropped fly ball) of the Kuala Lumpur Federal Territory, Datuk Hisham Yahya, said a divorce pronouncement delivered via cell phone was valid. So did Mr. Shiaffudin Sarawan in Singapore's Sharia Court. In a nutshell, and I quote, "Declaring a desire to divorce via SMS has the same effect as through a letter; this goes for declarations through the telephone or e-mail. Thus any wife who receives a divorce declaration should report it to the Sharia Court." Thus spake Mufti Hisham in the 7 July 2001 edition of *The Muslim News, Online Edition.*

According to this gaggle of experts, text-messaging divorce must meet four conditions in order to stick. First, no stand-ins or ghostwriters please; the husband must be the bona fide sender of the "I divorce you" message. Second, the husband must really, really, really want a divorce. No April Fool's jokes allowed. Thirdly, the phrasing should be clear and the intent unmistakable by the soon-to-be ex-wife. And last, but not least, receipt by the wife must be verifiable. That's all there is to it.

Hell Hath No Fury

As one might expect, Muslim women got mighty upset over text-messaging divorce, and even Will Shakespeare knew a woman scorned is bad news. Since Muslim wives in the Near and Far East can't exactly write their senators, they needed a spokesperson. Meet Sharizat Abdul Jali, Malaysia's outspoken Minister of Women and Family Development and big-time upholder of Muslim women's rights. She said the Mufti muffed it. According to Ms Jali, the idea of cell phone divorce "taints the sanctity of marriage and is demeaning to women," and she wants the whole dang thing reexamined by the country's Muftis' Council—Malaysia's supreme Islamic body. Bottom line—she's pushed for an official decree banning text-messaging phone divorce throughout the Muslim world. After reading accounts of Ms Jali's crusade, this writer hopes she never finds out members of the male gender like to drink milk straight out of the carton or pass gas at the dinner table.

Since she began her campaign, Ms Jali has gained serious support for her cause. This writer's contacts in Malaysia say Jali went straight to the Malaysian Institute for Islamic Understanding, a leading government think tank, and commissioned a study. Experts here released a statement to the effect that an SMS divorce does not reflect the spirit of the law. One government official, while admitting an SMS divorce is technically possible, dismissed the practice as just plain rude. In the end, Malaysian authorities, with lots of help from Ms Jali, banned text-messaging divorce in late July of 2001. In an official ruling, the government stated that while SMS divorces are possible, under Sharia law, a simple text message does not satisfy all the rules of divorce. The hubbub, dear reader, continues.

The Phone Company

Where does the phone company stand on the e-divorce controversy? An executive with Maxis Bhd, Malaysia's largest cell phone outfit, was quick to condemn the practice of text-messaging divorce. He said the practice is an example of how modern technology fails, and that some things that are important in life have to be done face to face.

Now THAT sounds like your everyday, sensitive, caring, empathetic telephone company executive. What planet is this guy from? Whoever heard of a phone company bigwig who was not willing to exploit the human condition for the sake of making a buck. I'm betting that right now some software engineer somewhere is working on the next generation cell phone. Features will include voice mail, global roaming, wireless web, and divorce-ur-wife—all at no extra charge.

One final note—the couple in Dubai who started the whole text-messaging SMS divorce brouhaha buried the hatchet and are living happily together with their infant son. Seems he didn't mean it after all.

Computer Factoid

fac · toid \fak' toid'\'   *n:*a single fact
or statistic variously regarded as being
trivial, useless, unsubstantiated, etc.

Bet You're Glad You Didn't Say That

Sooner or later everyone says something dumb. For most us the things we say aren't captured in print for posterity to remember. Not so for the rich and famous. Here are some of the stupidest things ever said about computers by people who should have known better.

"The analytical engine will never go beyond a theoretical possibility."
—Charles Babbage, inventor of theoretical machine based on modern computing principles, 1883.

"It would appear we have reached the limits of what is possible to achieve with computer technology, although one should be careful with such statements; they tend to sound pretty stupid in five years."
—John Von Nuemann, computer scientist, 1949.

"Computers in the future may weigh no more than 1.5 tons."
—*Popular Mechanics*, forecasting the relentless march of science, 1949.

"I have traveled the length and breadth of this country and talked with the best people, and I can assure you that data processing is a fad that won't last out the year."
—Editor in charge of business books for Prentice Hall, 1957.

"I think there is a world market for maybe five computers."
—Thomas Watson, Chairman of IBM, 1958.

"Computers aren't going to get much faster."
—Dr. Arthur L. Samuel, "The Banishment of Paper-Work," *New Scientist*, 1964.

"Computers are multiplying at a rapid rate. By the turn of the century there will be 220,000 in the U.S."
—*Wall Street Journal*, 1966.

"What is the microchip good for?"
—Attributed to an engineer at IBM's Advanced Computing System Facility, 1968.

"Most computers will probably still occupy a large room, however, because of the space needed for the ancillary software—the tapes and cards to be fed in, the operating staff, and the huge piles of paper for printing out the results."
—Professor Desmond King-Hele, *The End of the Twentieth Century?*, 1970.

"There is no reason for any individual to have a computer in their home."
—Ken Olson, President of Digital Equipment Corporation (DEC), 1977.

"So we went to Atari and said, 'Hey, we've got this amazing thing, even built with some of your parts, and what do you think about funding us? Or we'll give it to you. We just want to do it. Pay our salary, we'll come work for you.' And they said, 'No.' So then we went to Hewlett-Packard, and they said, 'Hey, we don't need you. You haven't even got through college yet."
—Steve Jobs, founder of Apple Computer, 1975.

"640K ought to be enough memory for anybody."
—Attributed to Bill Gates, founder of Microsoft, year unknown.

"I don't think it's that significant."
—John Roach, President of Tandy Corporation, commenting about the introduction of the IBM PC, around 1982.

"Each Fortune-type corporation surveyed had an average of 70 microcomputers installed; and the number of micros installed would grow at nearly five per cent each month until the end of the year."
—Results of Canadian Business Survey, 1983.

"I predict the Internet will soon go spectacularly supernova and in 1996 catastrophically collapse."
—Bob Metcalf, *InfoWorld*, 1995.

"Microsoft has stretched itself so thin, within a couple of years it will experience serious reversals. We'll make the millennium by deadline.'
—Bob Lewis, *InfoWorld*, 1997.

And Along Came Y2k

"The more I read, the more convinced I am that some economic disruptions are inevitable. The year 2000 problem is a serious threat to the global economy. Yet it isn't being taken seriously enough."
—Edward Yardeni, *Computer World*, 1997.

"I recently sold our New York City apartment and bought a house in a small town in New Mexico."
—Ed Yourdin, consultant, 1998.

"The Year-2000 phenomenon is clearly such a jolt, and we believe that it will me much more pervasive and serious than most of the disasters we've experienced in modern history."
—Ed and Jennifer Yourdon, *Time Bomb 2000!*, 1999.

"The Millennium bug might be God's attempt to confound our language, jam our communications, judge us for our sin…"
—A video produced by Reverend Jerry Falwell, 1999.

"Plague will follow shortly. Most of the inhabitants of the Northern Hemisphere will die within a matter of a few weeks, from cold, disease, fires started in an attempt to keep warm or violence. This is bad enough of course, to qualify as a disaster ranking with the Black Plague, if not the extinction of the dinosaurs."
—Cory Hamasaki, DC Y2k Weather Report, July 1999.

Isidore: Patron Saint of the Internet

Has that Internet browser of yours been acting a little strangely lately? Maybe you've noticed steamy, pea soup goo oozing from your keyboard when you try to visit Amazon.com? What's that eerie voice coming from your speakers? "Demy. Demy. Why you do this to me Demy?" Mmmmmm. This may not be the Melissa virus after all.

If you have been thinking that it is time for a little heavenly help with all these inexplicable Internet demons, you may be in luck. According to the Catholic Community Forum (www.catholic-forum.com), the Vatican has given the Internet its very own patron saint. The honor goes to Saint Isidore of Seville. Pronounced Ee-see-dro, he should not be confused with St. Isidore of Madrid, patron saint of farmers. The matter was finalized by group called the Internet Observation Service working for the Pontifical Council for Social Communication.

St. Isidore was a catholic bishop who lived in Spain from 560 A.D. to 636 A.D. He was the See of Seville, which at the time was the Spanish capital. Being a See (the early word for bishop) meant Isidore was the spiritual and intellectual leader of the Spanish people, but in those days this was easier said than done. At the time Spain was ruled by the Visigoth (or Goths), a race that tended to spend more time raping and pillaging than curling up with a good book or joining discussion groups. St. Isidore organized and presided over a series of powwows called the Councils of Seville and Toledo. As a result of the Fourth Council of Seville, seminaries and schools were established to counteract the growing influence of Visigoth barbarism. Saint Isidore's schools promoted the study of Greek,

Hebrew, liberal arts, law, and medicine. Through his work, Isidore is credited with breaking the Visigoth's hold in Spain.

Even though St. Isidore had a pretty good track record with the Goths, this really isn't why he got tagged for the Internet job. St. Isidore was a prolific writer. Although he is not known for original thought (e.g., St. Augustine, Thomas Merton, Benny Hill, etc.) or his independent writings, St. Isidore did have a knack for categorizing all knowledge known to man. Shortly before his death, Izzy completed his *Etymologiae*, twenty books cataloguing and describing everything from medicine (book 4) to beasts and birds (book 12) to victuals (book 20). The Catholic Encyclopedia describes the *Etymologiae* as being "clear, concise and in order." The work was reprinted four times over the next one thousand years, with the last edition produced in 1803. Modern experts have noticed something clever about St. Isidore's encyclopedic work. The *Etymologiae* is organized in a hierarchical fashion, and is described by many as the first example of a functional database. I guess this means St. Isidore could be considered the first database programmer, though no one can say if he had a pocket protector or wore hiking boots to work. An encyclopedia of all knowledge organized into a database by a geek in funny clothes—sounds like the Internet to me.

The St. Isidore nomination was not without controversy. Early rumors accused the Vatican's webmaster, a Spaniard, of lobbying heavily for the selection of his fellow countryman. Two other saints were also being considered for the Internet gig. One group was pushing St. Regalado, a fifteenth-century priest who was supposed to be a superb navigator, and is known for his ability to appear in more than one place at a time. A faction from the Spanish region of Catalan cast their votes for St. Tecla, claiming her image had been seen curing computer viruses. At one point St. Tecla's supporters reportedly set up a Web site for online confessions. Among the sins that could be forgiven were mail bombings and not paying for shareware. Alas, this writer, anxious to be forgiven of past shareware abuses, was unable to locate St. Tecla's website.

St. Isidore of Seville
(Bartolome Murillo, *St. Isidore* c. 1645, Cathedral de Sevilla)

Now that St. Isidore of Seville is the certified, sanctified, bona fide patron saint of the Internet, things should really start happening. Servers are going to stop crashing, and curses will be piled on the heads of email spammers. One source interviewed by this writer believes St. Isidore could even be solicited to reduce the sinner's time in Purgatory by every second spent waiting for a Web page to load. This possibility could not be corroborated with Vatican officials.

If you're anxious to get started with St. Isidore, there are a couple of things you can do. Pick up a glow-in-the-dark St. Isidore statue from Cardology Gifts (www.cardology.com) for only $4.95. According to the documentation, setting this baby close to your machine should "...help against slow downloads, error messages, etc." The Catholic Forum Web site (www.catholic.org) recommends calling on St. Isidore with the following prayer before beginning to surf:

Almighty and eternal God,
who has created us in Thy image
and bade us to seek after all that is good, true and beautiful,

especially in the divine person
of Thy only-begotten Son, our Lord Jesus Christ,
grant we beseech Thee that,
through the intercession of Saint Isidore, bishop and doctor,
during our journeys through the Internet
we will direct our hands and eyes
only to that which is pleasing to Thee
and treat with charity and patience
all those souls whom we encounter.
Through Christ our Lord. Amen.

Vatican programmers are rumored to be writing a version in C++. I understand that a Flash plug-in will be required.

fac · toid \fak' toid'\'   *n*:a single fact
or statistic variously regarded as being
trivial, useless, unsubstantiated, etc.

How to Hide a Secret Message in a Digital Picture of Your Dad and a Catfish

In the corrupt spirit of Enron and WorldCom, I'm offering you a bribe to read this factoid. Drop me an email and I'll send you a secret message hidden in a digital photograph of my dad and a catfish. Read on for details.

The technique of hiding information is called steganography. Here's how it worked three thousand years ago:

Suppose you're a general in ancient Greece and you're stirring up a rebellion against those pesky Persians. You've got to get a secret message to your spy in the Persian court. Being a big shot general, you're not going to do something stupid like travel to Persia yourself, so you need a worker bee to carry the message for you. Your first idea is to write your instructions in a secret code and have the messenger carry the note through enemy lines. There are a couple of problems with this strategy. If the enemy captures your man and finds the message, things could get ugly. Even if the Persians can't decode the message, the mere presence of a letter saying something like "44lethc *&m=o,e" will raise some eyebrows. Given enough time, the enemy might even crack your code. Worse yet, they could torture the messenger until he reveals the message and the secret code. A better approach would be to hide the very existence of the message.

You have a brainstorm. You sit a fellow on a stool, shave his head, and tattoo the message on his noggin. When his hair grows back, you send him through the enemy lines with the Persians none the wiser. The fellow gets his head mowed again when he reaches the good guys. Your secret message is delivered safely. Your armies win and the Persians are sent packing. By the way, the story is true.

The Greek general's name was Histiaeus, and the messenger was his servant. This was the first recorded use of steganography.

Tattooed messages on bald heads are one thing (the Germans used the same technique in World War II), but the digital world has given steganography and hiding data a whole new meaning. Large files like digital pictures and music are common vehicles for hidden messages. Let's hide a message in a simple .BMP image file.

Now You See It

Hiding data in a digital image or audio file uses three principles—large file size, the presence of "noise," and last but not least, the frailties of human perception. You already know large file sizes and digital images go together like Bugs and Elmer. Noise is the presence of digital inaccuracies. This occurs because the digitization process cannot make an exact copy of the source. Noise is said to be at an acceptable level if the inaccuracies cannot be detected by the human eye or ear. In a digital image of a photograph, noise is in the form of closely-packed colors and intensities. Remember those "frailties of human perception"? When it comes to digital images, we're talking about the inability of the human eye to pick up noise—very slight alterations of color, contrast, and brightness. These three factors are the foundation of the Least Significant Bit or LSB method of hiding data in an image. We'll talk about LSB, but first comes the lingo of steganography.

A *cover-object* is the data file that will hold the secret message. For spies and lovers, a cover-object is something large but harmless. The embedded-object is the message that will be hidden using a *stego-key* or algorithm. Depending on the method, the embedded-object could be a graphic, straight text, formatted file, or encrypted message. A *stego-object* is the new file carrying the embedded-object. Generally speaking, the steganographic process goes like this. A cover-object and embedded-object are selected. Both are submitted to the *stego-key*, and voilà—the process produces a *stego-object* that appears (don't forget those human frailties) identical to the cover-object. Now back to our digital image and the Least Significant Bit method.

Let's say our image uses true color. This means each pixel is described by three eight-bit bytes. In its binary form, Pixel #456 might look something like this:

01011101   10111010   11011001

Byte #1   Byte #2   Byte #3

The noise range is the cumulative effect on the senses of all bytes contained in the image. Taken alone, Pixel #456 is only a very tiny speck of color. Now take a look at the furthest right bit of each byte. This is the Least Significant Bit or LSB, because changing its value has the smallest effect on the total numeric value of the byte. It's the same with the human eye. Changing the Least Significant Bit will have an imperceptible effect on the image. The LSB is the hiding place for our message.

An LSB *stego-key* takes the digital equivalent of our embedded-object and stores the message across the least significant bits of many pixels in our digital picture. The new Pixel 456 looks like this:

<u>01011100</u>   <u>10111011</u>   <u>11011000</u>

Byte #1   Byte #2   Byte #3

Of course, depending on the message, the LSB may or may not get changed. In any event, the result is a new digital image (the *stego-object*) that looks exactly like the original picture (*stego-cover*). Yes, you've fiddled with a bunch of bytes and their bits, but the noise range of the new image has not been perceptibly altered. You now have a secret message hidden in an innocent digital picture, all without shaving a single head.

Picture Holding a Secret Message
(Image created by the author)

More Stego Stuff

The sequential LSB *stego-key* is one of simplest steganography techniques around. It's easy to detect because storing a hidden message in sequential LSB's creates a statistical pattern that differs from the unaltered portion of the image. For this reason, stego-geeks have developed other methods for hiding data. Storage of the message can be spread over the entire image using random byte selection. This minimizes storage abnormalities. In palette-based images like JPEG files, both the image and the accompanying palette can be altered. Of course, digital pictures aren't the only vehicles for hidden messages.

Audio and video files have massive levels of imperceptible noise. Changing tone bits and the pause duration between notes are great places to hide a love note to your surreptitious sweetie. Data hiding techniques for written text change spacing and the placement of individual characters. Even large hard drives on PC's can be used to hide data. File systems like FAT or NTFS allocate blocks for storage. Most of the time these blocks have unused space where secret messages can be stored.

I could go on and on, but if you want to read the definitive work on hiding information, pick up *Information Hiding: Techniques for Steganography and Digital Watermarking*, edited by Stefan Katzenbeisser and Fabien A.P. Petitcolas. Before you run down to your local Barnes and Noble, let me warn you—list price for this two hundred-page baby is eighty-five smackers.

Here's the Deal

As promised, I've hidden a secret message in a picture of my dad and a catfish. To retrieve the message you'll need a piece of freeware called "BMP Secrets" written by a company called Parallel Worlds. You can download "Secrets" from:
www.pworlds.com/products/i_secrets.html.

Send your email address to kirk.kirksey@operamail.com. I'd like to know your city, but if you think this is too much information, I understand. I'll send instructions along with a file holding a secret message. When you successfully decode my secret message, you must call my editor and praise my insight, wit, and skill. Demand that he give me a huge raise or else you'll return this book for a refund. Good luck.

Computer Factoid

fac · toid \fak' toid'\'   *n*:a single fact
or statistic variously regarded as being
trivial, useless, unsubstantiated, etc.

The Fungus Among Us

Aficionados of the 1950s Japanese sci-fi flick will fondly remember Godzilla, mother of all one-hundred-foot lizards, who was hell-bent on devouring Tokyo. A few years later (somewhere around 1962 I think) Norman "Spirit in the Sky" Greenbaum composed and then had the gall to record an hallucinogenic tribute called "The Eggplant that Ate Chicago." I never wanted to eat moussaka again after hearing that tune. If you're thinking large lizards and hungry aubergines will eat just about anything, hang on to your hat. Doctors in Michigan and at MIT have discovered a computer-eating fungus. And if fuzzy stuff in your circuits isn't bad enough, scientists in the jungles of Belize have turned up another saphoryte capable of snarfing the metallic surface right off your Norman Greenbaum CDs.

Desperately Seeking Fungi

According to a story published in May 2001 by the BBC, twenty-three computers were placed in the ICU of McClaren Regional Medical Center in Flint, Michigan. Not long after the machines were installed, Dr. Gregory Forstall, director of infectious diseases, noticed something a bit out of the ordinary. "We saw that the computers had a vent with a cooling fan," said Dr. Forstall, "and there was some sort of exhaust coming from the fan, and so when we took samples from the grid and from the room, we found there was a growth of several types of yeast and some filamentous mold." One of the molds Dr. Forstall identified was caused by a fungus called Aspergillus fumigatus.

Just after after Dr. Forstall's discovery, computers in one of MIT's labs began acting up. Help desk technicians threw in the towel and called in the experts. Upon close examination, it appeared that circuits and internal cables were in an early state of organic decay. Organic decay? How could this be? Rot is strictly a biological process requiring moisture, air, and (here's the strange part of this story) food. Microbial biologists studied the problem, and guess what they turned up—Aspergillus fumigatus—the same fungi found contaminating Dr. Forstall's ICU computers.

More on Mold

Most of the time, fungus travels the world as a spore—a sort of hard-shelled, microscopic seed. Fungus spores can be found just about everywhere; on furniture, walls, carpets, and heating ducts. Mostly a spore is just looking for a permanent home. When it lands on something moist and warm, it sets up shop and enters what scientists call the "fruiting stage." Your mother has another name for fruited fungus. She calls it mold, and why the heck haven't you gotten rid of that piece of turkey yet?

Some places seem too cold and inhospitable to sustain any sort of life, fungus or otherwise. Take the inside of a typical computer, for example. Pop the hood on your desktop, and about the only things you'll find inside are metal, green resin stuff, dust, and heat. Reminds me of my honeymoon.

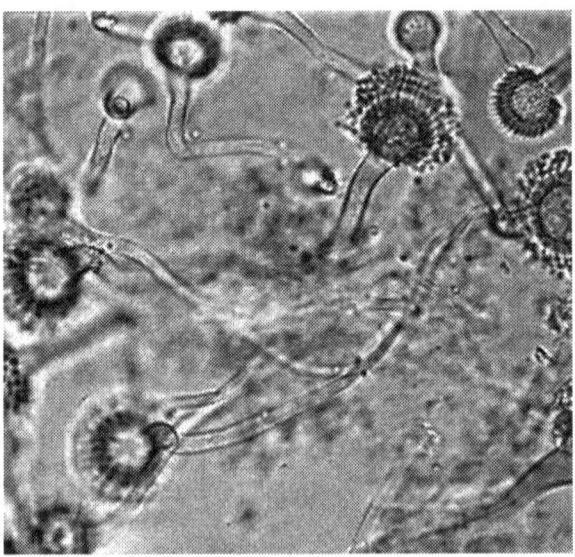

Aspergillus fumigatis

The key to the fungus-in-the-computer mystery is what you don't see. Aspergillus and his cousins are quite frugal, and are able to scrounge enough sustenance from nutrients embedded in the plastic polymer insulation found between the machine's microcircuits. In theory, this material is supposed to be a combination of inorganic plastics and resins. During the manufacturing process, however, molecules of organic-based contaminants get mixed in the polymer batter. After the whole thing is cooked and molded, these tasty bits become food for fungus.

Chomping on Your CD

And if circuit-chomping fungus wasn't bad enough, a couple of scientists have now discovered a fungus capable of eating the metallic surface right off your CDs and DVDs. For this story, we go to the jungles of South America.

After visiting Belize, Dr. Victor Cardenes of Madrid's National Museum of Natural Sciences noticed one of his CDs didn't look quite right. To make things worse, the platter was unreadable. A look-see under the microscope revealed the platter's aluminum and polycarbonate layers had been eaten away, and there was something else. Dr. Cardenes noticed some teeny tiny teeth marks.

Petri dish in hand, Dr. Cardenes took samples and, before you know it, he had a thriving colony of fuzz. This time the culprit was Geotrichum candidum. Like its distant cousin, Geotrichum was able to sniff out organic contaminants in the CD's polycarbonate resin. Snacking fungi nibbled through the binary number pits, turning Dr. Cardenes's CDs into a set of matching coasters.

When it comes to computer—and CD-eating fungi, you can't fool these fungus spores. A number of Aspergillus species are able to grow indoors, usually in dirty heating ducts and contaminated potting soil. Aspergillus fumigatus, the type of fungus fond of Dr. Forstall's computers, is classified as a weak pathogen capable of causing an infection called Aspergilloses in certain individuals with weakened immune systems. The CD cruncher Geotrichm usually lives in plants and animals, but occasionally can cause respiratory problems in humans. Your mother was right; cleanliness is next to godliness.

Bad News Good News

At first glance, a computer-eating fungus doesn't sound good. Never mind toxic pathogens and respiratory infections, I've got anonymous chat rooms and my Iggy Pop CD collection to worry about. But scientists tell us there is an upside to this story. Discarded computer equipment, including CD platters, is beginning to choke our landfills. Strains of computer-gobbling mold might be the answer for a little environmental housekeeping. See Mom, mold isn't all bad.

fac · toid \fak' toid'\'   *n*:a single fact
or statistic variously regarded as being
trivial, useless, unsubstantiated, etc.

Nerd: An Etymology

Nerd. We know one when we see one. He's the guy who drives the Porsche, but can never manage matching socks; the poor schmuck you don't dare speak with at cocktail parties unless your printer is broken. He is Bill Gates, billionaire with the $6.00 haircut. "Nerd." Where did this human label of the computer age come from, and why does it mean what it does? The truth is stranger than fiction. "Nerd," like computers, has traveled a long way in a very short period of time.

Most word gurus believe Dr. Seuss invented the word 'nerd' in his book *If I Ran the Zoo*, published in 1950. According to the etymology citation in the *Oxford English Dictionary*, this is the earliest documented use of the word. Here's the Dr. Seuss passage:

> "And then, just to show them,
>
> I'll sail to Katroo
>
> And bring back
>
> An It-Kutch
>
> A Preep
>
> And a Proo
>
> A Nerkle
>
> A Nerd
>
> And a Seersucker, too!"

Not all experts agree completely with the Dr. Seuss Theory. Slang maven J.E. Lighter says Dr. Seuss may have created 'nerd' as an adaptation of 'Mortimer Snerd,' the name of Edgar Bergen's cantankerous dummy. Lighter, editor of *The Random House Historical Dictionary of American Slang*, cites a 1941 publication using "Mortimer Snerd" to mean a "technical, brainy type of guy." Another scholar, Robert Chapman, suggests "nerd" may have come from surfer or hot-rodder lingo, and could come from 'nerts' or 'nuts'. Others believe nerd comes from 'nurd,' which began as 'knurd'. An article in the IEEE Spectrum (4/95 page 16) claims 'knurd' is 'drunk' spelled backwards, and is a word used to ridicule teetotalers. Last, but not least, there is D.L. Gold's theory. Gold figures "nerd" is probably a gentle version of "turd."

Not long after the Dr. Seuss book, "nerd" began showing up in the printed word—oddly enough first in Scotland. In 1957 Glasgow's Sunday Mail (February, 10) gave the definition, "Nerd—a square." "Nerd" pops up again in a 1961 skit at Swarthmore College called, "The Dean's Office." The character, college student Millard Fillmore Nerd, must painfully admit to the dean that he has broken no rules; alas—he's a square. The 1968-70 edition of *Current Slang*, published by the University of South Dakota, gave this definition; "Nurd—someone with objectionable habits or trait; an affected person…An uninteresting person, a dud."

When "nerd" became associated with computers is unclear, but the *Nerd Dictionary* (http://www.compnerd.com/nerd9.htm) supposes that the word entered the cyberculture sometime in the early seventies. About ten years later, "Nerd Pride" buttons began showing up in the hacker community. In the late eighties MIT students crossed GNU (an open source UNIX-like movement started in 1984) with "nerd" and came up with their own spelling—'gnurd.' In the nineties, professors Gerald Sussman and Hal Abelson created (and even trademarked) the "Nerd Pride" movement on the MIT campus. Sign up today and get your own Nerd Pride button, baseball cap, and—you guessed it—pocket protector.

fac · toid \fak' toid"\'   *n*:a single fact
or statistic variously regarded as being
trivial, useless, unsubstantiated, etc.

Microchip Graffiti and the Bill Sux Hoax

For the true computer geek, the equivalent of a girlie magazine foldout is a wall calendar sporting a microscopic photo of a microchip for each month of the year. When it comes to photographing these babies, Mike Davidson had the best job in the world. He was the creator of the *Chip Shot Calendar*. Each year, Davidson, a senior research engineer at the National High Magnetic Field Laboratory at Florida State University at Tallahassee, lined up his 'models,' chilled the champagne, donned his crushed velvet smoking jacket, and got ready for a strictly-private affair photo shoot with his high-powered Nikon FX/L optical microscope. Yeah baby, yeah! Every December, nerds across globe licked their chops as they hotly awaited his collection of the year's most curvaceous microcircuits.

Chip Art Exposed

In 1996, Davidson had lured an especially attractive MIPS R4000 chip to his studio and was about to go to work. His subject "got comfortable" and Davidson set the Nikon on low magnification—somewhere between 25X and 100X. This got the entire chip into the frame. To make the circuitry "pop up" for richer detail, he lit areas with a tungsten-halogen light, then bumped up the magnification to 600X and began to scan the surface looking for those especially tantalizing areas. As he scanned the geometric precision of microcircuits and junctions, Davidson suddenly stopped. On the surface of the resin wafer, Davidson could clearly make out a face. The rough kisser had glasses, a lumberjack hat, flyaway hair, and bore an uncanny resemblance to Waldo of "Where's Waldo" fame. Davidson shook his head and looked again. The face was still there.

"I realized it wasn't part of the integrated circuitry," said Davidson, "but I thought it might be something engineers had put on the chip to thwart anybody trying to reverse engineer it."

Intrigued by his discovery, Davidson posted the image on his Web site and soon was contacted by the chip's creator, one Kevin Kuhn, chip designer at MIPS Technologies, Inc., in Mountain View, California. Kuhn had worked long and hard on the chip, and had etched the face (this was a portrait of one of Kuhn's colleagues, not Waldo) in the resin as a sort of artist's signature. He explained to Davidson that chip art was a well-known practice among chip designers. Like programmers who hide secret functions in their codes (see the Easter Egg factoid), chip engineers are fond of adding a personal touch to an otherwise sterile product.

Davidson had stumbled into the world of chip art and found a new passion. The Chip Shot Calendar—forget about it. The engineer began searching for chip art, and over the years has amassed an impressive collection. He has found portraits of Groucho and Dilbert; a wedding announcement; planes, trains, and automobiles; sexy women; messages to lovers; and more.

There's a huckster selling fake Rolex watches on the wafer of an HP PA-RISC 7100 LC. Engineers at Lattice Semiconductor decorated their ispPAC30 with a "can o' worms" to symbolize problems encountered during the project. One of Davidson's most unusual finds came from the Cold War era. In those days, Russian designers were reverse-engineering chip designs created in U.S. companies. Digital Equipment engineers decided to send their Russian colleagues a message. Look closely at the MicroVAX 3000 and 6200 chip, and you'll find, written in Cyrillic, the Russian phrase, "VAX—when you care to steal the very best."

Since Davidson first revealed the shadowy world of chip art, the practice has become well known. Davidson's Silicon Zoo (http://micro.magnet.fsu.edu/creatures/index.html) features over three hundred examples of chip art. A reverse-engineering outfit in Canada called Chipwork features a collection of recent works at their Web site (www.chipworks.com/art/silicon_art.htm). Even the Smithsonian has a small collection of historical chip graffiti (http://smithsonianchips.si.edu/chipfun/graff.htm). With chip art in the mainstream, no one was surprised when an unusual specimen of chip graffiti made the rounds of the Internet. On the chip's surface, engineers at Intel had delivered a not-so-subtle message to Microsoft founder Bill Gates.

Microvax 3000 chip with Message to
Russian Engineers
(Image courtesy of ChipWorks)

Bill Sux

In 1998, this story hit the Internet:

API—Time Magazine reports an interesting case of high-tech graffiti. It seems that a couple of Intel engineers working on the design of a recent version of the Pentium microprocessor included a message that describes their feelings about Bill Gates, president of Microsoft, a good corporate pal of Intel's.

When a portion of the Pentium chip is examined under a powerful scanning electron microscope, the phrase "bill sux" is clearly visible, etched into the surface of the chip. The "flaw" in the chip was only discovered by accident well after the chip was released into the market, too late for Intel to prevent the chip from being used in the manufacture of tens of thousands of PCs.

Intel says that both engineers responsible were former employees of Motorola, makers of the chips that are the heart of the Apple Macintosh.

Both engineers have since been fired by Intel.

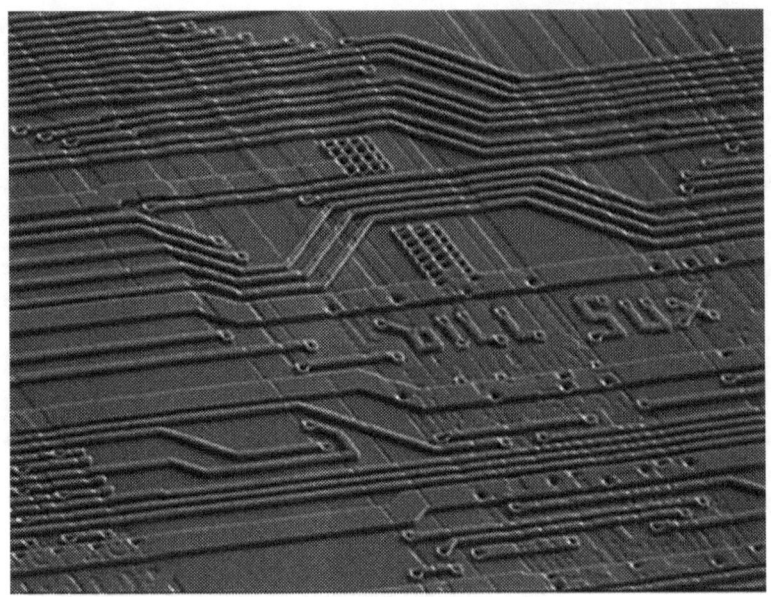

The Bill Sux Microchip
(Original source of this hoax image is unknown)

The piece was universally accompanied by either a graphic or a link to http://www.idt.mdh.se/kpt/billsux.jpg. Yep—right there on the chip, as clear as the nose on your face, was the message—Bill Sux.

Thousands of Web sites across the globe published the story. A blurb about the Bill Sux chip was even carried in the prestigious *Wired Magazine* (July 31, 1998). Unfortunately, the world had been duped. Bill (or at least Microsoft) may suck, but the chip art story was a hoax.

Most people today believe Apple zealots were behind the humbug. For one thing, the message takes a potshot at Apple lovers' two most despised icons—Bill Gates and Intel. Emotions aside, let's look at more tangible evidence. For one thing, the story is nowhere to be found in the *Time* magazine archives. The API reference is also bogus. There is AP (Associated Press) and there is UPI (United Press International), but there is no wire service called API. API in this case is probably a clever play on the Microsoft programming facility called Application Programming Interface, or API. Last but not least is the graphic itself. Pranksters lifted the circuit from the cover of Dr. Darrell Duffie's book *Dynamic Asset Pricing*, a backdrop. In his article "A Very Small Hoax," computer scientist Alan Peacock of Brigham Young University says he used a graphics freeware program called The GIMP to move things around and create a similar image.

I suppose the moral of the story is clear. Don't believe everything you read, even if it is printed on a silicon wafer.

COMPUTER FACTOID

fac · toid \fak' toid'\'   *n*:a single fact
or statistic variously regarded as being
trivial, useless, unsubstantiated, etc.

Spud Server

You can fry 'em, mash 'em, bake 'em, boil 'em, or tot 'em. You can turn them into soup or cook 'em in your frittata. Shell out $10 for the well-known kiddie toy, and you can dress them up with plastic eyes, ears, and moustaches, then set them on little red shoes and have your very own four-inch version of Edgar, my ex-brother-in-law. You know what I'm talking about. Potatoes. Spuds. Idaho apples. Personally, when I think of a batch of 'taters,' I think of little golden strips, glistening with artery-clogging grease, globbed with luscious dollops of ketchup and sitting next to a bacon burger from Hole-in-the-Wall (Dallas—Harry Hines Blvd., just south of 635). But I'm no visionary like Fredric White of Arlington, Massachusetts. Mention spuds to Fred and he immediately thinks "computer power." That's why in the summer of 2000, White built the world's one and only Web server powered by five rotting potatoes.

White, a double E graduate from MIT, got the idea after those wild and crazy guys over at "The Temple ov thee Lemur" (http://totl.net) who claimed they had developed the world's first spud-powered Web server. Even though the Lemurs churned out a lot of gratuitous hype and fooled some pretty heavy media types—the BBC for example—their "Potato Powered Web Server" turned out to be just another Internet hoax. Mr. White, for whatever reason, decided he would take the Lemurs' idea and run with it.

He started by looking for a non-traditional source of power. According to White, "any moist, soft, acidic object would do." A bottle of Jolt Cola was on White's early list of candidates, first because the elixir is highly acidic, and second because of the stuff's "hacker appeal." "Citrus fruits," said White, "work well, but are too expensive and too tasty to waste." He settled on the humble potato, mostly because potatoes are the traditional choice for powering small devices. As an example, White cited the "Two Potato Clock" which is commonly found in science museum gift shops. Rotting potatoes supply the equivalent of a battery's electrolyte, in this case a mild phosphoric acid. In a very pleasant email exchange, this writer suggested using Twinkies as a power source. Mr. White wrote back saying Twinkies would probably dissolve the zinc and cooper electrodes. I've got to go on a diet.

For the server's CPU, White selected a 16F876 model processor manufactured by Microchip. This baby's clock speed is a blazing 76.8 KHz. According to White's numbers, the low-powered CPU, paired with a 1.5V voltage supply, draws about 20 micro watts or "roughly 100,000th to 1 millionth the power of any Intel 386 board." There is a caveat to all this potato power. Technically speaking, spuds were only used to power the CPU. The serial port, which consumes two hundred times more juice than the CPU, uses a triple A battery. Converting the serial port to tater power would require an additional 1,000 rotting spuds; a situation Mr. White says he could not bring himself to face or smell.

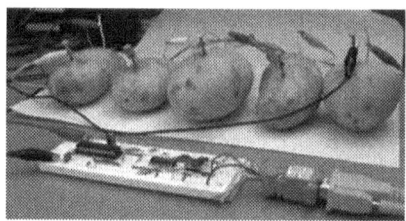

Spud Server
(Image courtesy of Fredric White)

The Spud Server connected to the outside world at 4800 bud—er—baud. Every five minutes or so, an external PC measured the voltage, current, and power output of the spud batteries, then sent the information to the Spud Server. System RAM is updated with the battery information and tater power consumption figures are displayed as part of the Spud Server's home page. How long will potato power last? White's first batch lasted fourteen days and three hours, at which time he was seeing "some definite sprouting action," as well as imminent putrefaction of Spud No. 3.

Alas, all good things must come to an end. Fredric White grew tired of sharing his workbench with five rotting tubers, and dealing with the pungent aroma of putrefying spuds. White pulled the plug on the potatoes, and converted his server to a single triple A battery. Who could blame him?

COMPUTER FACTOID

> **fac · toid** \fak' toid'\'   *n:*a single fact
> or statistic variously regarded as being
> trivial, useless, unsubstantiated, etc.

Rage Against the Machine

Hard drive crashes.
Network 'glitches.'
Spreadsheet files disappear for no apparent reason.

Be honest. Have you ever wanted to beat the living daylights out of your computer? Don't be ashamed. You're not alone, especially if you live in England. Officials in the British manufacturing division of Compaq Computers noticed that aggressive behavior aimed at computers and corporate computer departments was on the rise in the British Isles. After experiencing sudden computer errors, blokes and blokettes were seen cursing their computers, tongue-whipping technical support personnel, and, in some cases, bashing their hardware. To savvy yanks familiar with rush-hour commuting, all this cursing and bashing smelled a lot like All-American road rage. In 1999, Compaq commissioned Market Opinion and Research (MORI), a British research firm, to study the phenomenon of computer abuse.

Between March and April, 1999, MORI surveyed 1,225 computer users at 158 sampling points. In face-to-face interviews, respondents were asked a slew of open-ended questions about their computer experiences. Why did so many computer problems occur? What did computer support departments do to correct the problems? How did their colleagues behave when their computers failed? When the dust settled, patterns of computer abuse appeared.

In their report called "Rage Against the Machine," MORI researchers identified a growing problem they called Technology-Related Anger, or TRA. According to the Rage report, TRA arises from a head-on collision of the culture surrounding computers and pressures created in the workplace. "PCs are being marketed today as a commodity, implying that all one has to do is plug it in and turn it on." Unfortunately, computers and software are much more complex than TV commercials showing Internet grannies and cyber-savvy nuns thumping on keyboards would have us believe.

Bottom line…

Take a large dose of underestimated technical complexity, add the stress of employment urgencies and deadlines, throw in a what-the-!#*&-just-happened-to-my-spreadsheet error, and boom—you've got a bad case of TRA.

Here's what the experts say TRA looks like. Swearing at your monitor is not uncommon, especially if you're male. Verbally abusing innocent support personnel or cursing the IT department loudly in public are telltale symptoms too. If you're under the age of twenty-five, you might kick or shove your computer. If you're a woman, you're likely to jerk the plug out of the wall hoping to damage the evil contraption. There is method to this madness—or at least a pattern.

Dr. Robert J. Edlemann, author of the "Rage" report, identifies four Rage Profiles typifying TRA. "Abusive Annie" acts up at the first sign of trouble. She vents frustration easily and likes to shower verbal or physical abuse at her PC or IT personnel. "Controlling Colin" is a paranoid type and believes the PC is completely out of his control. He avoids the introduction of new technologies like upgrades. "Colin" won't go near a machine that he knows is not working properly, and of all the Rage profiles is most likely to completely destroy his computer when things go wrong. "Simmering Susan" is likely to be over fifty-five and blames herself when things go wrong. She will pout in silence until the pressure gets too much, causing her to explode. Last, but not least, "Analyzing Alan" will spend hours trying to solve his own PC problems, then blames the computer support department for missed deadlines. When he reaches his boiling point, "Alan" may resort to violence, but his actions tend to be concealed or underhanded.

Rage in the Office
(Origin unknown. Many believe this photograph is an Internet hoax)

When it comes to eradicating TRA, the Rage report isn't optimistic. TRA won't go away as long as businesses fail to evaluate real operational needs, and continue to overwhelm staff with new technology that doesn't deliver real savings in time and money. The next time you feel like taking a bat to your laptop, here are some suggestions from Professor Edlemann.

Take the Zen approach. Give the computer time to overcome the problem before taking action.

Take time to think about and work through the problem yourself. If you fail, don't keep trying.

If the problem persists, call computer specialists for support.

Don't stew over the problem. While waiting for the problem to be solved go on to other jobs. Finish vital paperwork, make phone calls, or read important documents.

Keep current backups of your work. If your computer can't be repaired, your work won't be lost.

Take a deep breath when dealing with computer support personnel. Treat them with respect. Understand their priorities and your own.

Remember—kicking, bashing, or unplugging your computer will only make things worse than they are now, and you could get fired to boot.

If you feel you've reached your boiling point, take a break. Get a drink of water; take a walk.

Think about your career. Swearing loudly in the office makes co-workers uncomfortable and could affect your next evaluation.

Don't take TRA home with you. Hurling vegetables at the children never repaired a crashed hard drive.

If you think you may have TRA and need professional help, you can reach Dr. Edelmann on a special helpline number. This writer predicts the international telephone charge for a British TRA counseling session will not make you feel much better about technology.

COMPUTER FACTOID

fac · toid \fak' toid'\'   *n*:a single fact
or statistic variously regarded as being
trivial, useless, unsubstantiated, etc.

Vendorese: A Translation

Anthropologists use the word "tribe" when referring to politically independent groups who share a language and culture. For many years, technology professionals have had continual contact with a loose collection of tribes called Software Vendors. Software Vendors may be small, with many tribes experiencing quick extinction each year. Peoples of the Dotcom Nation and Telecommers are recent victims of this phenomenon. Other tribes can be quite large and pervasive. In some cases confederations form, and resources are combined so that the hunt can be expanded. On the other hand, we have also witnessed full-scale war resulting in the complete annihilation of a rival Software Vendor tribe.

Despite our best attempts to observe and understand Software Vendors, very little is known about the inner workings of any single tribe. Here is what we do know. Software Vendors prefer no specific climate. They can be found in burning deserts, temperate savanna, and the bitter northern climes. Like peoples of the Indian subcontinent, Software Vendors have distinct structures of social class, and strict rules of behavior. Members of the worker caste, for example, are kept hidden—possibly because of their eccentric dress, poor hygiene, strange speech, and intense proclivity for Szechuan food eaten from little white take-out boxes. When granted an audience with tribal workers, it is best to bring along cheap trinkets. Coffee mugs, goofy pens, polyester backpacks, and stress balls in the shape of a human brain work well.

Members of the Hunter Caste also have distinct characteristics regardless of their tribe. Hunters are transient and mercenary, frequently switching their allegiance from one tribe to another for the sake of blood money. They are distinguished by expensive Italian loafers, and always have the unique aroma characteristic of after-shave abuse and the addictive use of breath mints. "Having Lunch" seems to be the Hunters' primary public activity. They are easily recognized by incessant travel (often forsaking family and friends) and an unexplained obsession for handing out business cards to anyone who comes within easy reach.

Perhaps the most distinctive characteristic of all Software Vendor tribes is their mysterious language. Although Software Vendors are anthropologically diverse, their dialect, called Vendorese, is commonly spoken and seems to be understood by all tribes. Akin to the Aztec stele or a Confucian scroll, Vendorese defies transliteration, remaining more like a collection of complex glyphs than a systematic corpus of words, phrases, or idioms. Scholars know little of its precise meaning. The following interpretations and translations have been made after spending dozens of hours in the presence hundreds of Software Vendor tribes. This work is not presented as proof of pragmatic translation, but merely as a starting point for more study.

Vendorese: A Brief Translation

"This is a fantastic idea. In fact, the enhancement you suggested is in the early stages of development back at our office."
Translation: I mentioned what you said to one of our programmers last Friday at Happy Hour. He wrote something on a napkin.

"You understand, these prices are for budgetary purposes only."
Translation: This will cost four times as much as these figures show.

"We've moved away from the traditional customer-vendor relationship. We prefer arrangements that position your company and ours as true partners."
Translation: We want to sell you the least amount of stuff for the most amount of money, and we want you to assume all of the risk.

"We bring a completely new outlook to this industry. Our perspective is as exciting as it is refreshing."
Translation: We lost our defense contract.

"In today's light-speed economy, our heuristic method of software development keeps you ahead of the competition."
Translation: We don't have a software development methodology. If we were carpenters we wouldn't use blueprints.

"We accomplish the function with a customized one-way manual interface developed by our programmers."
Translation: You've got to key stuff in.

"Our executive team is considering you as a beta site for our next release."
Translation: We've completed about half the programming. We don't have any documentation or recovery tools, and most of our support people don't know the system. We'd like you to use our product at your company and see if it works.

"All our software is created by our automated code generation system. This allows us to graphically define all logic and maintain an extensive data dictionary. Final modules are generated and linked using our exclusive link engine."
Translation: You won't believe how slow this baby runs.

"Our products use the latest Web *based technologies linked with automated content management databases. We fully exploit low-level hooks to operating system features as soon as they are made available to us."*
Translation: The system is written entirely by software geeks who don't know diddly-squat about your business.

"We will deliver the product you requested in 90 days."
Translation: We'll deliver the product in nine months.

"We will deliver the product you requested in the third quarter."
Translation: We'll deliver the product sometime after 2020.

"We will deliver the product you requested as part of our five-year strategic plan."
Translation: Forget it.

"You'll find our technological solutions completely unique."
Translation: We use a proprietary database designed by our CEO's cousin. Only seven human beings in the world can maintain this system. Three of them are on vacation this week.

"We'd like you to have a baseball cap, a coffee cup with our logo on it, and a set of glow in the dark shoelaces."
Translation: We think you're a tasteless geek with absolutely no decision making

authority whatsoever. If you were someone important, we'd give you a Mont Blanc fountain pen.

"I'm sorry I thought you understood that the price does not include monthly software maintenance charges."
Translation: There are hundreds of bugs in our code. We know where they are but haven't gotten around to correcting them yet. We'll charge you an arm and a leg to fix any errors that occur if you don't sign up for maintenance. Sorry, we can't be responsible for any damage to critical data. Have a nice day.

Translations offered here, although meager, are the result of incalculable hours spent with members of major Software Vendor tribes. Their literature and language have been analyzed, re-analyzed, and analyzed again. I have corroborated these translations with colleagues in the field, and have further verified their meaning by observing trade relationships both before and after goods have changed hands. Hopefully, linguists will carry on this important work, for there is much to learn. Vendorese is truly a mystery awaiting its Rosetta stone.

COMPUTER FACTOID

fac · toid   \fak' toid'\'   n:a single fact
or statistic variously regarded as being
trivial, useless, unsubstantiated, etc.

The Warhol Worm

For those of you who missed the attack of the Nimda computer worm, here's an idea of what it was like…

September 18th, 2001 8:15 A.M. Central Standard Time. The attack begins one week almost to the hour after the first WTC attack. Cyberterrorist or prankster? Only Dionne Warwick and the Psychic Network know for sure.

Massive internal Distributed Denial of Service (DDOS) bombardment begins. Workstations freeze. Firewalls crater. ISPs melt down. Small business Web sites are vaporized. Microsoft Web servers across the country become infected in record time. Corporate Internet connections disappear.

Six hours after Nimda begins and still there is no definitive virus fixes from Norton, et al. "Available Soon" says the Symantec Web site. C drives mysteriously set to sharable. MSNBC denies infecting the universe with their home page. Attorney General Ashcroft issues a press release. 'Edit the Microsoft Registry', he says. Wrong! Heated arguments in the restroom ensue. Who's dumber; government bureaucrats or Bryant Gumble? There's one Nimda version. No, two Nimda versions. No, count em, three Nimda versions. Microsoft's Web site says "download this patch. "Ooops, we're sorry this didn't work. We'll get back to you, but in the meantime, why don't you take out your credit card and reserve your very own copy Windows XP?"

General Electric is offline. Seimens, one of the largest Web sites in Europe, is off line. No one's answering the support line at Cissco. Still no fix from Norton, Sophos, or CERT. Odd—www.internettraffic.com routers on all continents show down status. Norton's Web site upgrades Nimda status from 'Easy to Clean' to 'THE END IS NEAR. Twenty-four hours later, infections worldwide are declining. *Information Week* says Nimda cleanup costs will exceed the $2.6 billion estimates for Code Red.

If you think the Nimda virus sounds bad—you had better sit down. The Warhol Worm is coming, and according to Nick Weaver, computer scientist at U.C. Berkeley, Warhol can bring the global Internet to its knees in less than fifteen minutes.

The Good Ole Days

Before we talk about the Warhol Worm, let's take a minute and travel back in time. Ten years ago rock-and-roll songs were hummable, CFOs didn't pierce their nipples, and everyone knew the difference between a computer virus, a worm, a Trojan horse, and a hoax. Strictly speaking, a computer virus is a malicious piece of software that spreads by glomming on to something else. Infected email attachments or evil Microsoft Word macros are well-known examples. A Trojan Horse, on the other hand, is a digital infection disguised as something else. NAKEDWIFE.EXE was a doozy. Click on this piece of work and instead of a dirty movie, boom—your 'C' drive gets erased. Computer worms are the scariest. In the digital world, a worm can self-propagate and execute without the aid of a host. No email attachments. No Word macros. No tempting names. Sophisticated worms even have the ability to create mutations and thus avoid virus hunters and virus detection software.

As if things weren't bad enough, there are the legendary virus hoaxes. Usually spread through the Internet, famous hoaxes have created at least as much hysteria as the real thing. Of particular note is the Irina Virus. Started in 1996, Irina was the brainchild of Guy Gadney, then head of electronic publishing at Penguin Books in England. Gadney was assigned the job of publicizing a soon-to-be-released sci-fi novel set entirely in cyberspace. As part of his PR campaign, he wrote a bogus letter to the press describing a deadly new computer virus named Irina (also the name of the novel) that was ravaging computers connected to the Internet. The letter was signed by one Professor Edward Pridedaux of the College of Slavonic Studies. Professor Pridedaux, one of the book's main characters, didn't exist, and neither did the College of Slavonic Studies. Global panic ensued anyway. So much for the notion of journalistic corroboration, but no matter—the Irina Virus, dear reader, is fodder for another factoid.

Fast forward to 2001. Viruses, Trojan horses, worms, and hoaxes are still around, but sometime around '94–'95 things had changed for the worse. As Ric Byrnes of Computer Associates likes to say, we've entered the age of the Cocktail Virus. As the name implies, the most deadly computer viruses today are polymorphic—they are a virus, Trojan horse and worm all rolled into one. Nimda is a good example. At the height of the plague, Nimda was able to download itself to vulnerable Microsoft servers (classic worm). Using Outlook address books, Nimda also created zillions of emails and became an infected attachment (classic virus). And last but not least, Nimda spread when users browsed to innocent-looking but infected Web pages (Trojan horse, sort of).

Fifteen Minutes of Fame

I'm thinking job descriptions for academic positions in major universities all have a section that reads something like this: "Dream up stuff that will scare the living heck out of normal people." If I'm right, Nicholas Weaver (nweaver@cs.berkeley.edu) of the University of California at Berkeley gets "Employee of the Year." Weaver (actually a graduate student at the time) has construed (but as far as we know, not actually written) something called a Warhol Worm. Named in honor of the sardonic quote of pop artist Andy Warhol, this insidious bundle of joy combines all the nastiness of its ancestors and then some. Here's how a Warhol Worm would work.

In the case of an old-fashioned computer worm, infection occurs one computer at a time because the worm scans a network address space looking for other computers to infect. Computer Number 1 becomes infected. From here the worm scans its immediate surroundings and infects Machine Number Two. Once the worm is in on Computer Number Two, both infected machines partition the address space and begin looking for new victims. Now there are two infected machines searching the Internet for vulnerable computers. Next there are six wormed machines, and so on. The plague rates follow this sort of pattern, and the number of infected computers rise exponentially as the worm finds its way into more and more machines. After a period of time, the infection rate starts to taper off because vulnerable computers around the world become harder to find. This is how the Code Red Worm spread. David Moore from Caida.org estimated Code Red infected around 350,000 computers in just under twenty-four hours.

The One-at-a-Time infection method is the old-fashioned worm's Achilles' heel. In the real world, most worms are stopped (or at lease slowed down) because major virus detection vendors like Norton or Sophos can formulate and distribute solutions faster than it takes a worm to infect all vulnerable computers on the Internet. Multiple delivery methods and self-mutation always make things harder, but, so far anyway, the good guys have always come out on top.

Here's Weaver's idea. Suppose somebody writes a computer worm that doesn't have to search for victims. Suppose the worm is programmed with the whereabouts of vulnerable computers BEFORE the infection begins. Weaver calls this 'hit list' technology.

A Warhol Worm could be supplied with a hit list of, say, 10,000 to 50,000 known targets, each with "a strong network connection and specific commercial interests." Hit list in hand (or at least in memory), Warhol is first unleashed on a dozen or so machines. From here, computers on the hit list are infected directly. No Searching Required. As each hit list machine is wormed, Warhol partitions the work by dividing the original hit list among infected machines. The smaller the hit list becomes, the faster computers on the Internet can be infected. Once all hit list computers are breached, the Warhol Worm resorts to traditional infection techniques and starts looking for stragglers.

Faster Than a Speeding Bullet

Weaver speculates that constructing a hit list would be a piece of cake. He cites evidence from the Honeynet Project (project.honeynet.org) showing that Internet 'scans' (automated Internet searches for vulnerable computers) are common, and for the most part, go unnoticed. What's even more troublesome, Weaver claims public servers could be targeted without scanning by using information readily available on the Internet.

Next, Weaver used a computer model to simulate the spread of a Warhol Worm. In a nutshell, he started with a 10,000 machine hit list, and assumed a population 1,000,000 vulnerable servers. Using these numbers, Weaver says the initial hit list could be processed in about a minute. After that, infected computers could perform100 scans per minute and take 1 second to infect a new machine.

Bottom Line:

According to Weaver's computer model, complete infection of a million vulnerable Level One servers on the Internet would take only 8 minutes, with a 99% infection rate occurring after only 6 minutes 30 seconds. To tell you the truth, I never figured out the Andy Warhol 15 Minute number. I suppose it really didn't matter, because Weaver's logic and numbers still scared the living daylights out me. If you don't believe me, you can read the Warhol Worm paper for yourself at www.cs.berkeley.edu/~nweaver/warhol.html.

Not to be outdone, three yahoos from Silicon Defense (www. silicondefense.com) have taken Weaver's Warhol Worm one step further. Stuart Staniford, Gary Grim, and Relof Jonkman call their creation a Flash Worm. Staniford et al speculate that a "determined hacker could have obtained a list of all or almost all servers with the relevant services open to the Internet in advance of the release of the worm."

As it happens, this writer read the Flash Worm paper (www. silicondefense.com/flash/), and I must say, Staniford and his buddies have a boatload of some pretty far-fetched assumptions. One of the biggies assumes a worm could be written and delivered unnoticed with a 45MB hit list (45MB is the address space required to target the 12 million Level One servers connected to the Internet today). Their conclusion—a Flash Worm carrying a twelve-million-machine hit list and using advanced vulnerability scanning techniques could kill the Internet in about thirty seconds.

Bullseye

When it comes to creating Warhol Worm targets, our friends at Microsoft aren't helping. As the MS shadow oozes over the known digital landscape, other products are forced out of the market. This creates an environment that's dangerously homogeneous. Whether it's apples, tulips, herds of cattle, or software, history teaches that diversity is good. As vulnerabilities in Microsoft products emerge, sameness across wide geographies means infections can more rapidly spread. Warhol and Flash Worms just make things worse—unthinkably worse.

Weaver sees four targets that are particularly ripe for exploitation by the Warhol Worm; Microsoft Internet Information Servers (IIS), Microsoft Exchange, various peer-to-peer file sharing programs (Napster-like imitators), and electronic messaging programs (AOL Messenger, MSN Messenger). IIS is particularly vulnerable because it's still the default installation for Windows 2000 servers, and provides a widespread and "highly homogeneous target." He's not alone. Shortly after the Nimda attack, one particularly caustic Gartner Group report advised switching to almost anything other than Microsoft's IIS product.

Of course infection is only one side of the coin. If twelve million computers get infected and nothing happens, so what? But a computer worm without a purpose is like a Big Mac without heartburn. Through the years we seen infected computers send political messages, wipe out boot sectors, destroy computer files, and create massive network attacks. Imagine hard drives in twelve million servers wiped clean, or worse yet, twelve million servers simultaneously emailing photos of my expansive ex-brother-in—law in a thong. I suppose yahoos in academia are supposed to dream up stuff designed to scare the crap out of the likes of you and me.

COMPUTER FACTOID

fac · toid \fak' toid'\`   *n:*a single fact
or statistic variously regarded as being
trivial, useless, unsubstantiated, etc.

The Death Door Riddle

While visiting the mall, you are drugged and kidnapped (that'll teach you). You awaken to find yourself in a room with two identical computers and two unmarked doors. A throaty voice tells you Computer Number One is programmed to only tell the truth. Computer Number Two is programmed only to tell lies. There are no markings to distinguish one computer from the other. The voice goes on to say that behind one door is a sudden and horrible death. The path to freedom lies behind the other door. Like the two computers, no markings indicate which door is which. You may ask one and only one question of either computer. What question could be asked that would lead you to freedom?

ANSWER: You would ask either computer which door the OTHER computer says is the door to freedom. The truthful computer is compelled to tell the truth leading you to the freedom door. Likewise the liar computer is programmed only to tell lies and must say which door the truthful computer would NOT point to. Regardless of which computer is asked, the answer would always be the freedom door. This, of course, assumes there are no bugs in the software. This could be a dangerous assumption if either machine is running Windows.

COMPUTER FACTOID

fac · toid \fak' toid'\'   *n:* a single fact
or statistic variously regarded as being
trivial, useless, unsubstantiated, etc.

The Trojan Room Coffee Pot

Way back in 1991, students and faculty in the Cambridge University Computer Science lab got their coffee from a solitary pot located in a third floor research area called the Trojan Room. Day and night, personnel from hither and yon trekked there for their java fix. A freshly-brewed pot of Trojan Room coffee didn't last long, and a high demand/low availability situation was fomenting a crisis. All too often blokes trudged down several flights of stairs, cups in hand, only to find a roomful of jittery caffeine addicts eyeballing an empty pot. Important research was being disrupted. World-renowned computer scientists suffered caffeine distress. Something had to be done because everyone knows a nerd without caffeine is trouble. When Quentin Stafford-Fraser and Paul Jardetzky tackled the problem, an Internet legend was born.

Stafford-Fraser worked on experimental ATM networks housed in the Trojan Room lab. "Being poor, impoverished academics," said Stafford-Fraser, "we only had one coffee filter machine between us, which lived in the corridor just outside the Trojan Room." The lab was outfitted with racks holding the computers used to test the network. An unused "frame grabber" was attached to one of the machines. Stafford-Fraser and Jardetzky fastened a camera to a retort stand and aimed it at the coffee pot. Wires from the camera were strung under the floor and back to the frame grabber. Jardetzky wrote a "server" program that captured images of the pot. Stafford-Fraser programmed a small "client" which could be installed on everyone's workstations. Every thirty seconds or so, Jardetzky's "server" captures an image of the coffee pot. According to Stafford-Fraser, "that was fine because the pot filled rather slowly, and it was only grayscale, which was also fine, because so was the coffee." All in all the system took about a day to write. Thanks to the work of two young engineers, every computer in the lab could now display an icon-sized picture of the Trojan Room Coffee Pot in the corner of the screen. Stafford-Fraser and Jardetzky dubbed their creation Xcoffee.

Xcoffee was a hit. Bob Metcalf wrote about the project in an article for *Comm Week* (27 January 1992). In 1994, the Trojan Room Coffee Pot was featured in a BBC broadcast. Other projects like XSandwichVan and XprinterOutputTray were planned, but sadly never implemented. Eventually the original frame grabber died and XCoffee nearly withered away. Daniel Gordon and Martyn Johnson found a new frame grabber and introduced XCoffee to the World Wide Web.

The Original Cambridge Trojan Room
Coffee Pot
(Image courtesy of Cambridge University)

Thousands of Netizens visited the Cambridge Trojan Room page, and hundreds of links point to the site. The Trojan Room Coffee Pot is the most famous coffee pot in the world, and spawned the Coffee Cam craze. The SLURP project at the University of Twente in the Netherlands has implemented a Distributed Coffee Information System (DCIS), allowing TIOS members to get coffee status information on their desktops. Faculty at the University of Australia in Sydney took the skinflint's way out and simply scanned in a picture of their espresso machine.

Perhaps the greatest tribute to the work of Stafford-Fraser and Jardetzky was RFC 2324—Hyper Text Coffee Pot Control Protocol (HTCPCP/1.0) posted as an April Fool's joke in 1998 on the http://www.rfc-editor.org/[1]. This officious sounding document (See http://www.faqs.org/rfcs/rfc2324.html for the full RFC) spoofs an Internet protocol for controlling "...all devices capable of making the popular caffeinated hot beverages (sic)." Among other innovations, RFC2324 lays out a new header field defining 'milk-type', 'syrup type' and 'alcohol type.'

Alas, all good things must come to an end. In 2001, the Computer Science Department at Cambridge moved to new digs. The coffee cam was discontinued, and the famous Trojan Room coffee pot that had been viewed by millions was in danger of being tossed out. Just in the nick of time, Cambridge officials decided to auction their piece of Internet history on eBay™. The most famous coffee pot in the world sold for $4,750.

---

1. RFCs (Request for Comment) are proposals for new or changes to Internet standards. All RFCs must follow format standards defined by the Internet Engineering Task Force.

COMPUTER FACTOID

fac · toid \fak' toid'\'   *n*:a single fact or statistic variously regarded as being trivial, useless, unsubstantiated, etc.

Weird On-line Museums Revisited

One summer many years ago, I vacationed with my Aunt Sadie. It was a memorable trip—a three thousand-mile travel trailer journey across our great country punctuated by stops at every obscure roadside "museum" we passed. You see, my Aunt Sadie believed to bypass a single fact concerning bootlace weaving (Nebraska), gypsum mining (Colorado), or the history of bowling (St. Louis) could seriously cripple a young man's intellect and potential for success in later life. "We're stopping," was my Aunt's battle cry in the war on ignorance.

Times have changed. Aunt Sadie is gone; her teardrop-shaped Shasta trailer with the much-hated plastic toilet bucket was auctioned to the highest bidder long ago. In her honor, I am pleased to present this Aunt Sadie Memorial pilgrimage to the most bizarre museums I can find. But cars break down and convenience store burritos give me gas, so I have forgone the vagaries of the highway and turned to the Internet.

Have a seat, buckle up, pop the top off your favorite cool drink. Here we go a-touring down the Information Highway looking for the strangest museums on the Web. Hang on tight because, like Aunt Sadie, we won't hesitate to U-turn across four lanes of oncoming traffic rather than pass up something interesting. First stop, an old favorite—a place dedicated to our own delusions.

Museum of E-Failures

http://www.disobey.com/ghostsites/
    "Dot Bombs"
    "Web Programmer—Will Trade JavaScript for Food"

"Page Not Found"

It's ugly out there. E-businesses drop like flies. More than half the winners of the coveted Webby Award have gone belly-up or been acquired. Web commerce incubators in San Francisco, Silicon Valley, and, yes Dell's backyard, Austin, Texas, look like ghost towns hit by the plague. Would-be zillionaires are papering their bathrooms with stock options and filing out applications for Home Depot. What the heck happened? Who knows, but curator Steve Baldwin is faithfully chronicling the downhill slide of what he calls the "Web's Great Gilded Age." In his Museum of E-Failure, Baldwin attempts to capture screen shots of defunct Web businesses before they are gone, never to return again. So far, he's got over eight hundred examples and the list keeps growing.

Roaming through Baldwin's collection, one is struck with one immovable impression—there were some pretty stupid ideas out there. How on earth did these people think they were going to make a living, much less get rich, doing this stuff? Still, strolling past images of so many broken dreams leaves one a little teary-eyed. Some sites' last gasp goes straight to the point. "Effective Immediately, Reciprocal, Inc., has ceased operations." Others, like Wrestleline.Com, a site dedicated to bringing die-hard pro wrestling fans the inside scoop, leave emotional missives sounding a lot like Juliet's final soliloquy to her husband. Their words speak of love, commitment, dedication, and moving on. Give me a break. On the other side of the coin, the Agillion.com site's (it is hard to figure out just what these guys were selling) last day gave no hint of trouble. They were simply gone. Last, but not least, are screen shots from those dying sites that unabashedly left numbers for interested investors to call. Some people just don't know when to give up.

The Moist Towlette On-line Museum

http://jsfrench.tripod.com/

You'll want to bookmark this baby. Curator John French has amassed an impressive collection of moist towlettes from around the globe, and perhaps beyond. Selections range the strictly utilitarian Medi-Pak Obstetrical Towlette and Mamo-Wipes, to a French, whimsical collection of Star Trek moist towlettes sporting pictures of Spock, Kirk, and The Enterprise. The international collection includes towelettes from Spain, China, and the USA Embassy in Sweden. For the technically challenged, the museum offers detailed instructions. "Tear Open Packet. Remove towelette and use."

Museum of Questionable Medical Devices On-line

http://www.mtn.org/quack/welcome.htm

Mark Twain once said he didn't like doctors because they winked at undertakers. After surfing through this place, he was probably on to something. Okay—bloodsucking leeches and poking holes in folks' skulls to let the demons escape—that's all ancient history. But what about a Foot Operated Breast Enlarger Pump? According to the Museum, four million people shelled $9.95 for this contraption in 1976 and all they got for their money was a pair of bruised boobs. Then there's the Stimulator and Crystaldyne Pain Reliever introduced in 1996. Wow. According to the manufacturer's claims, this baby could relieve headaches, back pain, arthritis, stress, menstrual cramps, earaches, sinus problems, nosebleeds, flu, and other ailments. At least twelve hundred people took the bait. Upon close examination, the Crystaldyne was nothing more than a barbecue grill igniter outfitted with finger grips. When used, the thing created sparks and caused a small electric shock. Not all gadgets are this amusing. The shoe fitting X-Ray unit was common in shoe stores across the country in the forties and fifties. The device was a fluoroscope with eyepieces allowing a shopper to "see" how a shoe fit before the purchase. Turns out these things leaked radiation like crazy and were outlawed in most states by 1970. The one housed at the museum was decommissioned in 1981. There's plenty more where these come from, so be sure to surf the Museum of Questionable Medical Devices just before the next visit to your doctor.

The Wolfman Jack On-line Museum

http://wolfmanjack.org/wolfman1.htm

Here's an on-line tribute to the legendary disc jockey. Not really weird—I like it because the Web site's designer misspelled museum in the HTML title code. It's "MUSEUM" not "MUSUEM," you moron.

The Toaster Museum

www.toaster.org

If you don't have enough excitement in your life, this URL's for you—an online museum dedicated entirely to the toaster. Imagine the thrill of seeing the Sunbeam 3816 or poring over the specs of a Procter Silex Bagel Smart Model 22430. A few minutes on this site and you'll never find yourself on the wrong end of a cocktail party conversation again. When a beautiful blonde finds herself wondering about the official definition of toast, you've got the answer. You'll tell her about the Maillard Reaction. Someone wants to know when the first toaster was manufactured—no problem. The day the boss announced he's taking the family to The Toaster Capital of the World, you're there with a roadmap and driving times. Sign up for the Toaster Newsletter and keep up with toaster fiction, HotPoint Updates, the latest toaster profiles, and more. Do your social life a favor. Stop reading this book right now and visit the Toaster Museum website. If the excitement becomes unbearable, try the Museum of Accounting History (http://accounting.rutgers.edu/SUMMA/SUMMA/subjects/acchis.html).

Proctor Silex with Silk Screen Panels
(Image courtesy of the Toaster Museum)

The On-line Museum of Shopping Lists

http://shoppinglists.bravepages.com/index.htm

The British don't have enough to do, and this site proves it. No wonder their economy is in the dumper. The curator, who understandably doesn't give his or her name, has collected discarded shopping lists from all around the British Isles. It's mind-boggling. Arranged by region, there are scanned images of long lists, short lists, weird lists, faded lists, rain-stained lists, and more. Peruse the collection and you'll find poignant prose like 'Froz Spuds', 'Bak Potatoes', and 'Bananas'. You can feel the desperation with the scribbled 'AA batteries.'

Museum of Menstruation

www.mum.org

I like visiting the Museum of Menstruation when THAT time of the month rolls around and I begin to wonder why that gal of mine would sooner bite the head off a field rodent than give me the time of day? The online Museum of Menstruation will go a long way in helping members of the male persuasion understand the cyclical mysteries of femininity. Believe me, guys, we've got a lot to learn And it's all free for the surfing. The list of MUM 'Site Topics' is nothing less than a wake up call to the male psyche. Look for a compendium of sanitary products including a complete history of the male-dreaded u-know-what (e.g. "Honey, would you go to the drug store and get me a box of u-know-what's?"). There's a Pad Directory, an Underpants Directory, a Tampon Directory, and even a Poetry Directory. Prominently displayed in the Essay Directory is Gloria Steinem's, "If Men Could Menstruate," in which she speculates men would inevitably brag about how long and how much (damn right, missy). Be sure to check out the Norwegian Menstruation Exhibit.

Don't be fooled. MUM is more than female plumbing specifics, unsettling paraphernalia, and male bashing. There's also Menstruation Humor link. "Did you hear about the guy who thought a sanitary belt was whiskey served in a clean glass?"

Museum of Non Primate Art

www.monpa.com

There are three sections or Wings to this online museum. Forget about 'Why Cats Paint', 'Dancing with Cats', and go straight to the Bird Art Wing. You guessed it—it's all about bird crap (they call it 'splay' but it's still bird crap) spatula'ed up from windshields, sprayed with chemicals, framed and dressed up as art.

The current online exhibition spotlights bird crap splats from Great Britain and Europe. Six splats are featured. The Barn Owl splat shows a "globular splash prone to considerable lobular extension on impact." In the splat of the kestrel, "The copious creamy envelope contains a handsome brown nucleus." A splat of mallard crap let loose on an overcast day with winds approaching 35 mph "…has the satisfying texture of oil paint freshly squeezed from a tube."

If you'd like to become a "Splay Enthusiast" and collect your very own globs of bird crap, the museum's "Splay Collection and Preservation" page tells you everything you need to know. Here are the highlights. Windshields traveling at 60 mph work best for collecting bird crap. After wiping off the glass, cover with a thin sheet of plastic to catch the crap when a bird craps. If you don't have plastic and a bird craps on your windshield anyway, don't worry. Stop the car. Wait until the skak or binding crust covers the entire piece of crap, then gently loosen the crap with a drop of oleander or witch-hazel oil. The bird crap is now ready for framing, and can be given to your brother-in-law for Christmas. If you'd like an animation of a bird crapping on your windshield, go to http://www.monpa.com/ba/splat.html. If you think collecting avian crap is for the birds, think again. Somebody in Dallas shelled out $6,000 for a dual splay of a blue-winged teal dated 1983.

Questionable Medical Devices, Moist Towlettes, Toasters, Menstruation and Bird Crap. Forget about the Interstate, it's all on the Web. Aunt Sadie—wherever you are, I hope you've got DSL, lots of cache and a high-res monitor. I love you.

fac · toid \fak' toid"\'   *n:*a single fact
or statistic variously regarded as being
trivial, useless, unsubstantiated, etc.

Electronic Brain Predicts Winner of Presidential Election

Computers entered the world of political elections in the 1952 presidential race between Democrat Adlai Stevenson and his Republican opponent Dwight D. Eisenhower. Stevenson's platform relied on a successful term as governor in Illinois and a well-known family name with a long political history. War hero Eisenhower ran as a "service to the country" candidate. From the early days of the race, national polls pegged Stevenson as the campaign favorite.

Even before the election CBS executives were looking for way to predict an early winner and give their network an edge in the ratings. In August 1952 a team from CBS News contacted Remington Rand's Eckert-Mauchly division. Company PR representatives claimed the company's Univac computer was a machine capable of accurately predicting election returns. The CBS election news team including reporters Walter Cronkite and Charles Collingwood traveled to Philadelphia to see the "electronic brain" for themselves. According to one story Collingwood arrived late to the meeting and the Univac sent a personal message to him via a nearby teletype machine. "Collingwood, you're late. Where have you been?" The CBS newshounds were convinced.

CBS hired Dr. Max Woodbury, a mathematician form the University of Pennsylvania, to develop software capable of analyzing vote counts as they were reported by the states. According to Dr. Woodbury the program produced a probability model based on a generating function driven by the number of votes reported by each state. On election night Dr. Woodbury was stationed at the Univac while Cronkite and Collingwood manned the CBS election headquarters. Cronkite was on the anchor desk. Close by was a teletype machine connected to the Univac.

Voting results were given to Dr. Woodbury as soon as they came in, and by 8:30 P.M. the Univac was predicting 100-to-1 odds in favor of Eisenhower (Dr. Woodbury states the probability as .997). Odds from the Univac seem to contradict exit polls and predictions by humanoid pundits. CBS executives decided not to announce the Univac's predictions to the audience. At 9:00 P.M. the electronic brain was putting 8-to-7 odds on an Eisenhower victory. Feeling the computer was now under control, CBS announced the Univac's prediction to the public. A moment later Dr. Woodbury discovered an error. He had accidentally added a zero to the number of votes reported for New York state. The mathematician corrected the error and reran his program. The Univac again predicted 100-to-1 odds for an Eisenhower victory, which remained in the 100-to-1 range for the rest of the evening.

When all votes were counted, the Univac's predictions (and Woodbury's software) were amazingly accurate. The Univac predicted Eisenhower would get 32,915,000 votes. Officially Eisenhower received 33,936,252 votes. The computer's prediction (remember this was 1952) was only off by about 3%!! The Univac's first calculation of the electoral vote count was 438 for Eisenhower and 93 for Stevenson. The official electoral count for Eisenhower was 442 with Stevenson receiving 89 electoral votes. The Univac's prediction missed the electoral numbers by only 1%!

In the end, Cronkite, Collingwood, and Woodbury accomplished their mission. CBS was the first network to successfully predict the winner of a United States presidential election. By the 1956 election all three television networks were using computers to predict the outcome of the presidential race.

COMPUTER FACTOID

fac . toid \fak' toid'\'   n:a single fact
or statistic variously regarded as being
trivial, useless, unsubstantiated, etc.

Confessions On-line

All good Catholics know just how inconvenient life can be after committing a heinous sin. I'm talking about confession. Oh sure, you feel good when it's over, but this confession-slash-repentance drill can easily eat up several hours that would be better spent watching the game.

In today's time-is-money world, it is no surprise that Catholics began turning to computers and the Internet for a little spiritual relief. After all, you can buy a car on the Internet—why not a clean conscience? In the name of time-saving convenience your *Factoid* investigator decided to survey the history and current status of on-line confession.

CD Confession

One of the first attempts at an automated confession system was promoted by an obscure German fraternity. Back in 1996 the Lazarus Society, a group describing themselves as a "non-profit ecumenical humanitarian organization" from Cologne, Germany, decided to make your trip to a clean conscience just a little bit easier. All you needed was a PC and the Society's software, Confession by Computer CD.

With Confessions by Computer, forgiveness was a point-and-click affair. As confession began, the sinner was guided through the appropriate prayer and recitations. From drop-down menus one or more choices from a pre-assembled library of two hundred sins were selected. A 'Contrition Engine' linked combinations of failings to one or more of the Ten Commandments then calculated a statistical weight derived from the gravity of the combined transgressions. Pretty cool, uh? Using this weight, penance was chosen and presented to the miscreant. Atonement could take place during the session or at a later time.

111

Confession wasn't the only feature of Confessions. The program delivered text and audio renditions of the prayers "Our Father" and "Hail Mary", as well as the text-only versions of fifty other prayers, the complete rosary, the order of the Catholic Mass, and a Protestant church service. Suggestions for contacting a carbon-based (human) member of the clergy were also included. List price of Confessions by Computer back in 1996 was 78 German Marks or about $52.00. Fourteen marks were donated to charity.

For plugged in E-Types of the new millennium, Confession by Computer seemed like a perfectly logical thing to do. Unfortunately the Catholic Church didn't buy it. Confessions died when the German Conference of Bishops issued a strong condemnation stating the software did not conform to the Catholic theology of confession, and could lead to a false understanding of the practice. According to a spokeswoman for the Conference, "you cannot have sins forgiven by the push of a button." From this writer's point of view, I don't know why not.

Confession Via URL

I admit the Confession by Computer CD is one big fat envelope pusher. But the Internet—now there's an obvious medium for clearing one's conscience. After all, the Vatican's Web site went live in 1997 (the site is run by nuns and operates on servers named after archangels). At least one bishop uses his Web site to recruit priests. Following the Vatican's lead, parishes all over the world jumped on the bandwagon. On-line confessionals popped up faster than Japanese tourists at a free buffet. One much publicized Cyber-Confessional was www. theconfessor.com. Father Louis Bernhardt in Alvin, Texas operated another popular on-line Catholic confessional.

Things changed late in 2002 when the Man in the Pointy Hat said confessing on-line isn't kosher. According to an official release, the Holy See warned Catholic bishops and priests not to use the Internet to hear "online confession." Seems Catholic bigwigs are worried about digital confessions being blackmail fodder for hackers. Pretty lame if you ask me.

Like most on-line confessionals, theconfessor and Father Bernhardt's sites were discontinued soon after the Vatican's tantrum. For those readers who are tormented by sin but are too lazy get in the car, I am happy too report a few locations remain. One site, www.beichte.de looks very devout, but unfortunately it's all in German. For all I know these guys could be telling you to go drink an imported beer. For an on-line prayer to St. Anthony try www.carosantantonio.it.

Yep, the site is in Italy, but offers an English version. Sorry, confessions are no longer available.

If you're in serious spiritual pain, pay a visit to http://agep.home.netcom.com/confession.html. At first glance, this looks like the real deal. The site begins with a solemn intro extolling the serious nature of confession. Further down you'll find a list of two dozen or so sins, some of which you may not realize you've committed. My favorite is "Did I give an unfair wage to my employee" (I think I'll send this one to my editor). You can enter you're email address and type in your sin. I am assuming you'll receive an email describing your penitence and request for a credit card offering. Unfortunately, the whole thing falls apart when you see a picture of Sister Mary de las Rosas. It's the face of a young woman sloppily pasted on the body of a three-ton, sepia-toned nun. I give up. I can only conclude on-line confession isn't happening.

Plenary Kiosking

One last hope for the technology-based confessional may just be Greg Garvey's Automatic Confession Machine or ACM. Garvey's idea is strictly a compromise position. The ACM doesn't use the Internet. Instead, the ACM sits in a real-live, sanctified Catholic Church. The thing would be a real eye-catcher sporting a red neon cross. The penitent would enter a booth made from gleaming black Plexi-glas. Using a mouse, transgressions would be from a pick list containing a menu of the Seven Deadly Sins and the Ten Commandments. A firmware based priest (no pun intended) asks the sinner a series of questions, taking special interest in sins of the flesh. Analysis is performed and sins are ranked by an artificial intelligence engine using gravity ratings. Penitence is printed on a handy, wallet-sized form and the sinner is dismissed.

The advantages of Garvey's approach are obvious, especially considering the current low status of Catholic priests these days. No risk here, since no priest/human interactions take place. Savings in lawyer's fees alone justify the system. And, using aggregate data collected by the ACM, the Catholics could easily spot 'sin trends.'

Sinners—don't put away your car keys. I can only conclude the Catholic Church has failed to utilize Cyberspace to alleviate the spiritual burden for common sinners like you and me. It's all very depressing. I think I'll go to a strip club and have a beer.

COMPUTER FACTOID

fac · toid \fak' toid'\'   *n*:a single fact
or statistic variously regarded as being
trivial, useless, unsubstantiated, etc.

Easter Eggs and Where to Find Them

You never know where something unexpected is going to pop up—like inside your favorite spreadsheet or word processor. It's true. Buried in the bowels of the world's most popular software products are messages, games, and diversions created by a crafty programmers. In high-tech parlance, these little gems are called Easter Eggs, and you can only find them if you know the secret instructions.

This idea of embedding secrets inside a product isn't new. Artists, authors, and filmmakers have been planting Easter Egg equivalents for hundreds of years. The Mona Lisa is said to be a self-portrait of the artist Leonardo Di Vinci. The dodo bird in Lewis Carroll's *Alice in Wonderland* is a reference to the author's difficulty in pronouncing his real name because of a stutter (Charles Do-Do-Dodgson). Alfred Hitchcock is famous for fleeting cameos in his own films. The arcane culture of computers has taken the practice to new heights.

One of the earliest computer-related Easter Eggs was created by author (and creator of the programming language FORTRAN) Donald Knuth. In the sixties, Knuth wrote his landmark work called *The Art of Computer Programming*. In Volume 2 entitled "Seminumerical Algorithms" the index contains an entry for "Royalties." Knuth's "Royalties" points back to a page describing an "organ-pipe distribution." This is said to reference the pipe organ in Knuth's home purchased with royalties from a previous volume of "Algorithms."

When hidden in software, an Easter Egg can be almost anything. An Easter Egg could be a statement. A few years ago, circumstances could cause a flight simulator from Maxis to display an image of men in swimsuits kissing. A disgruntled gay programmer reportedly created the Egg in protest of company policy.

Sometimes dirty jokes hide inside Easter Eggs. Here's one from Microsoft's Word 97. First, send the kids out of the room. Next, open a Word 97 document, and type each of the phrases shown below.

> I'd love to see you naked.
>
> I love porn.
>
> I am gay.
>
> Shag me.
>
> Ice boobs go with what?
>
> Love her and leave her.

Use the cursor to highlight each phrase, one by one. Once a phrase is highlighted, open the thesaurus (shift-F7) and see what you get.

Now, type zzzz and run Word's spell checker against it. Oh my!

◆   ◆   ◆

Programmers often use Easter Eggs to sign their work. Sometimes you'll just get a scrolling list of names. Other times you might get a full-blown, multi-media production. One of the grooviest Eggs around is called "Hall of the Tortured Souls" embedded in Excel 95. If you do things just right, you'll be able to see a picture of development team members. Here's how to do it. The following instructions were taken from Easter Egg for Dummies at http://www. dummies.com/eggs/excel.html.

1. Launch Excel 95 from the Start button, which automatically opens a new Workbook and a blank sheet. If Excel is already running, you can click the New Workbook button on the toolbar, or you can select File—>New and click the Workbook icon on the General tab.
    Whichever method you choose, you should wind up with a new open Workbook.

2. Use the down-arrow key, the Page Down key, or the scroll bar on the right side of the screen to scroll to cell A95.
    Cell A95 should appear to have a dark frame around it.

3. Click on the number 95 to the left of cell A95.
    All of row 95 is highlighted.

4. Press the Tab key.
    All of row 95 should be highlighted except for cell B95.

5. On the menu bar, select <u>H</u>elp—><u>A</u>bout Microsoft Excel.
    The About Microsoft Excel box appears.

6. Press the Shift and Ctrl keys; while you hold them down, click on the <u>T</u>ech
    Support button in the About Microsoft Excel box.
    Now you're inside Excel's 3-D Hall of Tortured Souls! Use the keyboard's
    arrow keys to move around the room; use the C and D keys to look up and
    down.

7. Proceed forward and up the stairs to see the names of the Excel development
    team as the names scroll along the stairway walls.

Another room is hidden inside the 3-D Hall of Tortured Souls. To visit this
room, follow these steps:

1. Turn away from the stairs, face the opposite wall, and type EXCELKFA.
    The wall disappears, and you see a treacherous, zigzagging bridge that leads
    to a second room.

2. Use the arrow keys to cross this narrow bridge safely.
    When you arrive at the secret room at the end of the bridge (not an easy
    task!), look around to see pictures of the Excel developers hanging on the
    walls!

To exit from all of this, follow these steps:

1. Click on the Close button in the upper-right corner of either room (or both
    rooms).
    The rooms disappear.

2. Click on the Close button in the upper-right corner of the About Microsoft
    Excel box.
    The About Microsoft Excel box disappears.

3. Click on the Close button in the upper-right corner of the Workbook's
    menu bar or select <u>F</u>ile—><u>C</u>lose from the menu bar to exit the Workbook.

4. To exit Excel, select <u>F</u>ile—>E<u>x</u>it from the menu bar or click the Close but-
    ton in the upper-right corner of the Excel window.

◆   ◆   ◆

Microsoft's development team for Internet Explorer 5 created a cute little slam
for the competition. Try this in IE5.

In the Toolbar go to Tools>Internet Options> Languages…
Click on 'Add'
In the 'User Defined Field' ad ie-ee
Click on 'OK'
Highlight the entry that reads 'User Defined [ie-ee]
Click on 'Move Up'
Return to IE
On the Tool Bar Select 'Search' then 'Customize'

Watch the IE5 logo clobber the dinosaur (probably meant to represent
Netscape's mascot Mozilla) hatching from the egg.

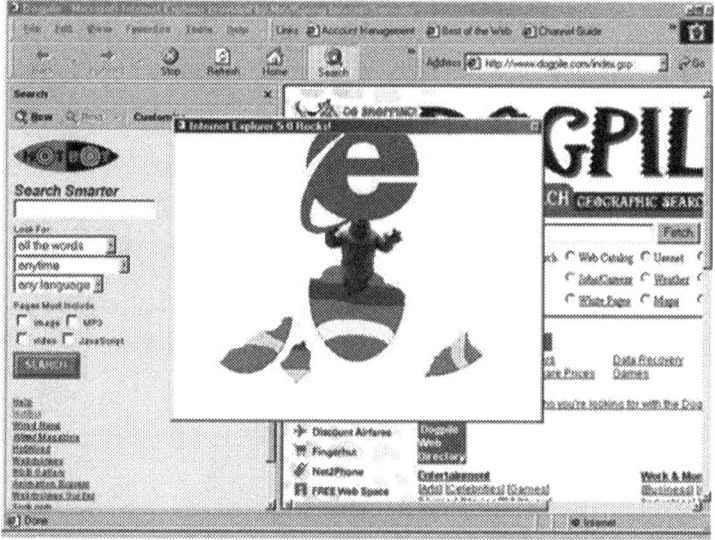

Explorer E Bonking Mozilla
(Image created by the author)

◆   ◆   ◆

Need a break from all that boring word processing work? Reportedly, there is code embedded in Word 97 that brings forth a pinball machine. WARNING: Reports of this Egg are everywhere but getting it to really work is tricky. Some Easter Egg hunters believe Microsoft engineers designed the Pinball Egg to succeed at random. Here's the code anyway.

Open a new Word 97 document
Type the word 'Blue' (with a capital 'B')
Use the cursor to highlight the word
Go to Format>Font and select 'Bold' and change the color to blue.
Click 'OK' and return to the document
Hit 'End' which brings you to the end of the word
Type a single space
Type a single quote (that's 'not')
Type a space and another single quote
Select 'Help' and 'About Microsoft Word'
Move the cursor the Word icon and Left Click
(Some Hunters say you must be holding Ctrl+Shift when you Left Click. Other say to hold Ctrl+Alt and Left Click.)

◆   ◆   ◆

Last but not least—the pièce de résistance, the Mother of All Easter Eggs. Remember all the moaning about the size of Office 95? There was even a cartoon showing an eighteen wheeler labeled "MS Office 95" making a delivery to a customer's house. Microsoft decried claims of bloated code and fell back on the sorry excuse—"enhanced functionality means bigger programs." The joke was on them. MS Excel 97 contained a hidden flight simulator. Here's how to find it. And by the way—this one really does work.

Open a worksheet and press F5
Type X97:L97
Press the Tab key
Hold Ctrl+Shift
More the cursor to the Toolbar and click on the Chart Wizard

Moving the mouse controls the tilt of the flight path. The right button goes forward; the left button reverse. Watch for the programmer's names inscribed on the mountain.

I understand why computer programmers want to sign their work. Pride in authorship is a high-minded quality. On the other hand, every time I run into a piece of software that is fatter, slower, and more expensive than it has to be, I wonder what it is I'm not able to see.

COMPUTER FACTOID

fac · toid \fak' toid"\' *n*:a single fact
or statistic variously regarded as being
trivial, useless, unsubstantiated, etc.

InterPet Explorer

Every scribbler worth his rollerballs has the First Commandment of Investigative
Writing tattooed on that particular part of the brain most often taken hostage by
first year journalism instructors. "By the third sentence of the first paragraph, the
reader should clearly understand the writer's intent." I'm going to break this rule
so bear with me.

In December 1898, Marie and hubby Pierre Curie announced the discovery
of radium. Although the Curies' discovery led to some of the greatest innovations
in medicine, too much of the stuff sent an over-irradiated madam a-glowing to
her grave (alas, some years before poor Pierre died after being run down by a
wagon loaded with army uniforms). Even though the duo had won the Nobel
Prize, the Curies can't take the credit. Their work relied on dozens of cast-off and
forgotten experiments marked down two-for-a-quarter in the garage sale of science.

It is a fact. The eventual value of seemingly useless knowledge can never be
predicted. Who knows where today's taxpayer-funded study of "ketchup viscosity" will lead. Think of it. A hundred years ago the Curies discovered radium and
today we have glow-in-the-dark panties. This very same mystery of knowledge
puzzle comes to mind when considering Dr. Irene Pepperberg and her colleagues
toiling those long hours at the MIT Media Laboratory. Dr. Pepperberg and her
team have written a Web browser for parrots called InterPet Explorer.

Polly Want a Cable Modem?

Here's the problem. According to Dr. Pepperberg, a visiting professor from Arizona, the eight million parrots living in America today are bored out of their
minds. This is as clear as the nose on your face. Every day Mom and Dad leave

for the office, and the kids hustle off to school. The house is a morgue and all Polly gets out of the deal is a little birdseed and yesterday's front page. "They [parrots] are like children," says Dr. Pepperberg. "They are left at home for eight or nine hours a day and this results in some strange behavior. Some chew their wings, others chew their feathers. It's not very healthy."

All of this avian angst caught Dr. Pepperberg's attention. Back in Arizona, the good doctor studied parrots for two decades and claims they are plenty smart enough to surf the Web. It seem parrots have a lot of brainpower. For their body weight these birds have really large brains, and on many laboratory tests perform as well as chimps and dolphins. Large brains and a socializing disposition mean parrots need a lot of stimulation to stay healthy. Dr. Pepperberg says the Web may be answer.

The team began by building a "smart perch" for an African Gray Parrot named Wart. Propped on his perch, Wart has easy access to a controller, a four-positioned joystick, and 17-inch screen, speakers, and a Web cam (this, by the way, is a better setup than I have in my cube). Using the controller and joystick, Wart can choose wallpaper or tunes from a jukebox. Web applications under development include a video and music browser, an acoustic mirror, live video feeds from parrots in the wild, puzzles, mazes, a kaleidoscope, and tools for remote interaction with the owner.

Scientists think there is a lot to learn here. They are not using Pavlovian reinforcement to entice Wart to surf. "All we do is show him the tools. He determines his own course of action. Wart's motivation for using the setup is the intrinsic reward of interaction, problem-solving, entertainment, and diversion—much the same for computer users." This brings up the relationship issue (e.g. S-E-X). What training will a newbie parrot need to create and sustain an on-line relationship? Will the on-line relationship lead to physical intimacy? I don't know about you, but I'd like to know the answer to that one.

InterPet and the Future

I can't stop thinking about the Curies and the eventual value of what today may seem like useless knowledge. Where will Dr. Pepperberg's InterPet Explorer lead us? Perhaps in a few short years we'll see a P-Commerce revolution complete with P-Mail and online P-Brokers. pBay will offer birdseed and gilded cages. You never know, Amazon Dot Com could become successful on name recognition alone and offer P-Bestsellers like *Green Like Me* and *Hell No I Don't Want a*

Cracker. And then there is P-Chat. "Hey baby—want to come over to my place an roll around on some clean newspaper?"

fac . toid \fak' toid'\'   *n*:a single fact
or statistic variously regarded as being
trivial, useless, unsubstantiated, etc.

Whacking Your Google

Close your eyes and imagine the perfect athletic activity for geeks. For starters, the contest must be completely virtual. No face-to-face interaction permitted, as this requires obsolete social skills like eye contact and pesky verbal communication. Players must be equipped with any Web-enabled device—laptops, desktops, wireless PDAs, or cell phones. Forget about demanding exercises and sore muscles. Touch-typing is the most strenuous physical activity needed. Penalty points accrue if a pregnant spouse, nearby orphanage blaze, or injured pet is able to distract the player. Last but not least, the game must be so devoid of practical value that office managers institute policies forbidding play on company time, yet enticing enough to create a global following of like-minded nerds, geeks, hackers, and digital misfits.

For something of this magnitude, only one venue will do. It's the Madison Square Garden of Cyberspace, the Las Vegas of the Internet, the Rose Bowl of the Virtual Beyond. I'm talking about Google, the Mother of All Search Engines, with over three billion indexed Web pages. Ladies and gentlemen. Boys and girls. Nerds and nerdettes. May I present Googlewhacking, the Sport of Kings.

GoogleWhacking

Even though the game's origins are foggy, one Gary Stock is credited with creating the sport's catchy handle. "All I did was name the thing," says Stock who tracks Googlewhacking results on his Website. We do know that Googlewhacking is only the latest in a long line of pointless Web sports. Remember Ego Surfing? You and a buddy put your own names in a search engine, and the one with the most hits springs for drinks. Then there was the ever popular Find-A-Date, in which contestants create bizarre personas (e.g., "I'm an unemployed, heavy smoker who loves moonlit walks in the sanitary landfill behind my mobile home.") on Internet matchmaking sites. The first player to receive a serious reply wins. Googlewhacking elevates these ideas to a loftier intellectual plane. At least that's how Stock sees it. "You've found yourself. You've found other people. You've caused other people find you. There's really nothing left to search but concepts," he proclaims. "You've evolved to a higher state." That's what Google-whacking, the game, is all about. Here's how it works:

Start the game by typing two separate terms in Google's search box. The terms, known as *Whack Factors*, must be single words only—no two-word phrases, quotes, or boolean arguments allowed. Hit the "Search" button. Your objective is to find one and only one Web page in Google's three-billion-plus Web page database. If, immediately after the Google search you see "Results 1-1 of 1", stand up and holler, 'cause baby, you've just found a *Googlewhack*.

If you think this is easy, let me give you an idea of just how tricky Google-whacking can be. I got eighteen pages with "crustacean literati," four pages with "vanadate lozenge," and get this, "escalator mustard" turned up 793 pages including someone who Googlewhacked this combination before me. Be patient. It can be done. Here are some noteworthy Googlewhacks from around the Web. "Flummoxed Pontifex" from www.jmagar.com turns up a page entitled "Popes for All Seasons." The whacker who first typed in 'apocrypha eviscerations' got a page about the End of Time. 'Epeus meandered' uncovered a BLOG (Web Log) by someone named Epeus who used 'meandered' in a daily entry.

Getting on the Whack Stack

Googlewhacking rules are fairly straightforward and, as you would expect, can be found at www.googlwhacking.com. There are only three. Rule Number One—Googlewhacking terms must be found in a legitimate English dictionary. It's hard to cheat on this one because Google spell checks every search term for you. How can you tell if you're whack is legit? When Google completes a search the blue bar above the results says "Searched the Web for." This is the list all of your search arguments. All underlined words are linked directly to www. dictionary.com. No line, no Whack. Rule Number Two—Google has the final say. If the result of the search doesn't read "Result 1-1 of about 1", try again you pathetic loser. Rule Number Three—No word lists allowed. Both *Whack Factors* must be included in a page of text. Bibliographies, dictionaries, thesauri, or stu-pid lists are all out of bounds. Once you've discovered a bona fide Googlewhack, you can log your find on googlewhacking.com's Whack Stack along with your

Hack (nickname) for all to see. At this writing, over 45,000 Googlewhacks have been discovered. Take it from me—there are some doozies.

IMPORTANT NOTE: Google's spiders don't crawl the Whack Stack. This means Whack Stack entries aren't used to create a second Web page for Google to find and index. However, if you include your Whack in the text of a Web page—say a personal Web Log (BLOG)—your Whack will be entered into the Google Index thereby preventing Whack Raiders from stealing your Googlewhack (I can't believe I'm writing this way).

Whack Scoring

Googlewhack scoring methods have created a bit of a controversy for whacking aficionados. Gary Stock stubbornly insists Googlewhackers have become "unpleasantly competitive," and that's not what the game is about anyway. Stock says scoring is irrelevant, but if you must score, his suggestion is simple. You get one point per Googlewhack; one point if the whack makes you smile; and one point if you learn something. That's it. Obviously, Mr. Stock isn't well-versed in the realities of human nature vis-à-vis the World Wrestling Federation and the NFL. Something a little more cutthroat was needed.

Early on, the idea of Googlewhacking was to use two <u>common</u> words to score—the more common the better. Following this train of thought, a whacker's score should reflect the simplicity of the search terms; the simpler the terms, the higher the score. Seems straightforward enough, but it took a while to come up with a sound scoring formula. Programmer Kevin Marks is credited with inventing the official Googlewhack scoring system. His method is based on the combined complexity of both terms as measured by the Google search itself. To determine the score of a Googlewhack using the Marks Method, perform a search on each individual Whack Factor. Look at Google's 'Results 1—10 of about <number of pages>' message. Note the 'number of pages' found for each term. Add these two numbers together (one for each Whack Factor), and violà—that's your Googlewhack score. The higher the number, the better.

In researching this article, I had the opportunity to interview, via email, several Googlewhacking experts. I wanted to explore the more subtle aspects of their craft. One Whacker who called himself Thorazine Tom employed Cut-Ups, a technique frequently used by the Beat writer William Burroughs (*Naked Lunch*) in the 1950s. Cut-Ups are quadrants torn from random newspaper pages that are rearranged to form new pages. Tom scanned his Cut-Ups looking for odd word combos. Another Whacker I'll call Sally laid several of her mom's magazines side-by-side on the floor. Each was opened to a random page. Sally dropped a yard-stick across the open pages, then followed along the straight-edge looking for possible *Whack Factors*. If you want something a little more automated, you can download Kevin Mark's Whacking Tool from http://homepage.mac.com/kevinmarks/whack.zip.

There's much, much more to report about Googlewhacking, but I've got to stop. It's just too depressing to think people spend so much time and effort on something this dumb.

COMPUTER FACTOID

fac · toid \fak' toid"\' *n:*a single fact
or statistic variously regarded as being
trivial, useless, unsubstantiated, etc.

The Irina Virus

>Subject: Virus Alert!
>
>Ladies and Gentlemen;
>
>FYI
>There is a computer virus that is being sent >across
the Internet. If you receive an e-mail >message with
the subject line "Irina", DO NOT >read the
message. DELETE it immediately. >Some miscreant
is sending people files under >the title "Irina". If you
receive this mail or >file, do not download it. It has a
virus that >rewrites your hard drive, obliterating
>anything on it. Please be careful and >forward this
mail to anyone you care about.

>(Information received from the Professor
>Edward Pridedaux, College of Slavonic Studies,
>London.) .

The Irina Letter

In September 1996 Graham Culey was a virus researcher for Dr. Solomon's Anti-Virus Toolkit. While attending a Virus Bulletin Conference, Culey's office received a flood of desperate phone calls. Frantic journalists described a new virus called Irina capable of wiping out hard drives and damaging a computer's CPU. According to the callers, Irina was rampant on the Internet and there was no known cure. Culey needed and answer and needed it fast.

The Irina Letter

From the start, Culey was suspicious. For one thing, stories about Irina closely resembled the Good Times virus hoax. True—word of Irina was spreading like wildfire through cyberspace, but virus sleuths couldn't put their hands on a single confirmed infection. Most of the circulating e-mail warnings were copies of the same letter referencing one Professor Edward Pridedaux from the College of Slavonic Studies in London. The College of Slavonic Studies didn't exist, and no one could locate a Professor Pridedaux in or around London. The more Culey investigated, the more he believed Irina to be a well-orchestrated hoax. He was right.

Stephen Baxter, a British math teacher turned science fiction author, had a respectable list of sci-fi thrillers to his credit. His latest tale was a completely new kind of work. Baxter's Irina was an interactive novel that took place on the Web sites of the story's main characters, Irina Zotova, and (you guessed it) Professor Edward Pridedaux of the College of Slavonic Studies in London. Baxter's publisher, Penguin Books in the U.K. would host Irina Web sites and handle publicity. The task of marketing the Baxter's book fell to Guy Gadney who headed Penguin's electronic publishing division. There had never been a novel like Irina, and Gadney wanted a PR campaign to match.

Just before the book's scheduled release, Gadney mailed bogus letters to newspapers and TV stations warning of a deadly virus being spread via an email message with the subject line Irina. Each letter was signed by the fictitious Pridedaux. According to a story in the *Daily Telegraph* (London), some newspapers received as many as six of Gadney's letters. There was never any mention "of a Penguin book, a publicity campaign or that the warning was a PR stunt." Frightened recipients began posting copies of the Pridedaux letter on the Internet and global panic soon began.

Culey quickly sniffed out the truth—Irina was nothing more than a PR stunt gone bad. He used the British press to blow the lid off the Irina story. Penguin quietly shut down the Irina Web site and issued a press release, but it was too little too late. Word of the Irina virus had already spread around the world. Guy Gadney was fired after crafting a snooty public statement that, according to the *Telegraph* story, "irritatingly glosses over little matters like culpability." In subsequent interviews for the magazine *Ansible*, Gadney claimed he had planned to send an explanatory follow-up letter after the phony Pridedaux warning, but was never given the chance. As for author Stephen Baxter: the novel Irina rarely appears on his list of credits.

COMPUTER FACTOID

fac · toid \fak' toid"\'   *n*:a single fact
or statistic variously regarded as being
trivial, useless, unsubstantiated, etc.

BowLingual

I sometimes wonder what is going through my dog Otto's head. At dinnertime is he thinking, "I'm getting sick of this stinking canned mush of pig entrails and would really like a top sirloin strip marinated in ginger soy sauce with a side of crispy chicken gizzards served on a nice clean China plate,"? Is sniffing another dog's butt and then licking me in the mouth the dachshund's conscience revenge for my sticking big globs of peanut butter to the roof of his mouth? These are the times I would like to know what Otto is thinking, and now it seems that maybe I can. In February 2002, Japanese toymaker Takara Inc. released BowLingual—a computer-driven contraption designed to help you interpret your dog's emotional state. So far this thing doesn't work on cats, hamsters or ex-wives—only dogs. It costs about a hundred bucks and is only available in Japan. Takara press releases say the company has sold over 200,000 of the things to Japanese dog owners. And I thought these people were in a recession.

The Dolittle Project

The BowLingual idea got started with inventor Robert Wayne Hamilton's Dolittle Project (yes, they spell it with only one "o"). If Mr. Hamilton hasn't already gone off the deep end, he is certainly standing on the diving board. Hamilton has credited himself with inventing something called the LSD Flight Simulator. He was also an early pioneer in the area of something he called Rubber Memory. When it comes to animals and the Dolittle Project, his idea is to enable animals to "actually talk using human speech." This would be accomplished with his "forthcoming Dog-Voice Collar." Once fitted with his invention, he believes talking four-legged critters would cuss out cosmetic company executives for using animals to test lipstick. I'll admit this would be an attention-getter coming from an eighty-pound Lab. According to the Web site stats, the Dolittle Project started in January 2001 and has six members—not exactly a groundswell.

Fast forward to August 2001, the date of Takara's first BowLingual press release. This document refers to BowLingual as Dolittle Project #01, but references to Hamilton and his movement are noticeably absent. No credit is given the man. Instead (according to the document), a three-way Japanese partnership has been struck. Japan Acoustic Lab will offer a "vast assortment of voiceprint and data analysis technology." Index Corporation will build the—get this—animal emotion analysis system. Takara and subsidiaries will develop and distribute the product. Here's how it's supposed to work.

Say What?

BowLingual comes neatly packaged with two pieces of hardware. One is a microphone small enough to clip to Fido's collar. The microphone transmits growls, woofs and barks to the owner's handheld console. Here's where the real magic takes place. The owner's console is about the size of a credit card and sports a small LCD. When the console receives a voiceprint, all kinds of fancy schmancy voice print analysis take place, and the dog's emotional state is categorized. Six emotional patterns are possible: Frustration, intimidation, assertion, amusement, sadness, and desire (watch out, Aunt Gladys's leg). The BowLingual engine searches a library of two hundred phrases that have been matched with the current doggy state of mind. The result gets displayed on the owner's console. For example, if you've put a sock over Fido's head and let him walk around the apartment bumping into furniture, his emotional state is likely to be 'frustration' and you'll see phrases like "I've had enough!" or "I can't take much more of this!" Pull the sock off, Fido's emotional state immediately goes to amusement and you'll see "I'm happy" or "Oh, yeah!" But that's not all.

BowLingual further analyzes Fido's voice patterns, which are stored in three different modes. I'm sure these lose something in the translation, but here they are anyway: Happiness Level Diagnosis, Friendly Level Diagnosis—and my favorite—the Bow Wow Diary. Using these tools will tell you if you've raised the canine equivalent of Charles Manson or the Dali Lama. The Happiness Level Diagnosis supposedly measures levels of Fido's assertion, satisfaction, frustration, and aggressiveness using a scale of one to five doggy stars. Watch out. If puppy wants something and you're not cooperating you may get: "Please, please! If you don't I'll whine."

Of course, doggy socialization is very important. If you've noticed Fido wanting to tear off the head of the Chihuahua next door, check out the Friendly Level Diagnosis feature. Feelings of animosity and affection are scored on a point system. A high score means you've got a well-adjusted pooch and can avoid inconvenient therapy appointments and expensive doggy Zoloft. As I stated earlier, the Bow Wow Diary is my favorite BowLingual feature, because we all want to know how our pet's day has gone. Bow Wow Diary does the trick. Through the day, emotional data is stored in three different time categories: morning, afternoon, and evening. BowLingual software turns this information into a diary format with over 120,000 combinations. If you see "Today was a happy day" or "I had a great time playing with my tennis ball," pat yourself on the back. You've created a pleasant and intellectually-stimulating environment for your pet. Although certain phrases haven't been programmed into BowLingual, you'll know Fido has probably been reading *Russell's History of Western Philosophy* while you were at work. On the other hand, if you see something like "It was so boring today. Nothing special happened," get ready to be sued by some offbeat canine anti-boredom protection group.

That's not all. The product also comes equipped with a doggy gesture analyzer. What is described as a dictionary-like function allows the owner to register specific doggy gestures. When triggered by the owner, the console registers the gesture, and an audio description is played out of the unit's speakers. Future releases of the product will see BowLingual Mail that will deliver Fido's message via the Internet. Instead of AOL's familiar 'You've Got Mail' notification, I'm hoping BowLingual Mail will say, "You've got a New Stain on Your Couch."

I'll admit it. When I first read about BowLingual I thought it might be cool to know what was running through Otto's brain. It would be good to know if the little stinker was well socialized, had his aggression under control, and if he had a good day. But then I pondered BowLingual's price tag. I can buy a lot of peanut butter for $100.

fac · toid \fak' toid'\'   *n*:a single fact
or statistic variously regarded as being
trivial, useless, unsubstantiated, etc.

The Brava Computerized Bra

My Uncle Ralph used to say he never met a pair of bazoongas he didn't like. I'm sorry to report that Uncle Ralph has moved on to that Gentlemen's Club in the sky, but here's something he would really like. It's called Brava, and it is the world's only computerized bra. When I first heard about this contraption, I wondered why the world needed a bra controlled by an embedded microprocessor with a modem connection. The answer is simple: Brava is designed to make a good pair of bazoongas even better.

Suction Junction

Each year, American women spend zillions in the quest for bigger breasts. "Enhancement" methods run the gamut from hocus-pocus to scientific. A cream made from something called Pueraria mirifica, found only in Thailand, claims to deliver results in just four weeks. Some breast-enlargement pills boast even faster results. Surgery can deliver immediate gratification as well as a larger cup size. Iffy results can be expected from the more exotic products, and the dangers of breast enlargement surgery are well known. According to its inventors, the Brava computerized bra lets women avoid risky surgery and strange voodoo, yet delivers results that have been scientifically proven. Here's how it works.

The Brava bra starts with two hard plastic cups (in Brava lingo these are called "domes"), which are fitted to the patient's breast size. Each ya-ya is completely encased in a dome, which is lined with suction cups, thus ensuring an airtight seal against the patient's torso. Cabling encased in soft tubes connects the cups to a "computer pack," Brava's trademarked Smart Box. Inside the Smart Box are microprocessors and software that this writer hopes is not based on anything from Microsoft. The rechargeable Smart Box is about the size of a deck of cards and fits snugly between the two domes in an inter-cleavage pouch. Wrap the whole thing in a black mesh sports bra, and you're ready to get started getting big, or bigger, whichever the case may be. Oh yeah, I almost forgot. The Smart Box also contains a modem, but we'll talk about this later.

Flip the On switch, and Brava starts doing what it does best. Computers in the Smart Box begin regulating suction, and air is pumped out of the domes. A mild pulling action is created, gently drawing the breasts forward. As long as the computer is working correctly, Brava sustains this constant pulling. I shudder to consider the effects of a software bug or, perish the thought, a Brava virus introduced by a competitor.

According to Brava inventor Dr. Roger Khouri, the device uses a method known by reconstructive surgeons for thirty years. The technique is called tension-induced tissue growth. This method is used to lengthen limbs, and in the implanted tissue expanders used in breast reconstruction for cancer patients. The idea is simple. Cells in breast tissue like to be crowded. Stretching tissue using suction creates gaps between cells. In response, cells begin to replicate in order to close these gaps. More cells mean more tissue, and more tissue means bigger breasts. (Note to Austin Power's fans: I know what you're thinking, but the International Man of Mystery was cheated when he bought his famous penis-enlarging pump. Tissue "down there" is too elastic and will not respond to tension-induced tissue growth.)

Dome Land

When Dr. Khouri first presented the results of Brava at the 1999 annual meeting of the American Society of Plastic Surgery, things did not go well. Even though he had studied twelve Brava women, the good doctor was met with belly laughs and bad jokes. In a follow-up study, Dr. Thomas J. Baker used Dr. Khouri's protocols. Dr. Baker's subjects were measured before, during, and after their use of Brava. Eighteen months later, magnetic resonance imaging (MRI) studies confirmed that the study subjects' breast growth was not caused by irritation or seeing a photograph of Brad Pitt. No scar tissue. No increase in fat. No temporary swelling. Brava worked. In the end, the good Dr. Khouri had the last laugh. Brava passed clinical trials with flying colors, and the FDA has blessed the device for marketing. At around $2,500, Brava isn't cheap (the company offers financing plans).

Before whipping out your VISA and taking the first step to Hooter Nirvana, there are a few things you need to know. First, Brava isn't for everyone. If your profile resembles Dolly Parton, seek "fulfillness" elsewhere. The official blurb states that the "apparatus" works best for women whose cup size is A or B, and that patients can increase one cup size after the prescribed ten weeks of use. That's right—ten weeks. Breasts need sustained stretching to grow properly, hence the ten-week Brava cycle. During the ten weeks, Brava must be worn at least ten hours a day. According to some patients, this takes a little getting used to. A set of heaving mammaries can be distracting at the conference room table, so most patients wear their Bravas at night. Suction cups on the domes must maintain an airtight seal against the torso, forcing patients to sleep on their back. If the seal is broken, a loud alarm sounds and the suction stops. Remember the modem connection I mentioned earlier? Brava home office honchos want to be sure their device is used properly. The onboard modem transmits the duration of proper operation and any alarms recorded by the CPU. Even though patients may notice significant growth during the first six weeks of use, these early increases are due to swelling and tissue reproduction. As tissue enlarges, breast swelling subsides and cup size permanently increases. You can now convert your Brava domes to an attractive windowsill herb garden. If you think Brava may be for you or someone you know, check out the Brava Web site at www.brava.com.

Let me warn you—you'll find lots of tasteful pix of women's breasts. Take a look if you're not offended by such things. And if you run into my Uncle Ralph, tell him hello for me.

COMPUTER FACTOID

fac · toid \fak' toid'\'   *n*:a single fact or statistic variously regarded as being trivial, useless, unsubstantiated, etc.

Cap'n Crunch and the White House Toilet Paper Shortage

John T. Draper—hacker, phone phreaker, daddy of the Blue Box, and cyber legend extraordinaire. Draper's escapades with the phone company, phreaker groups, and the FBI are well known. Still, the truth about those glory days of phone hacking is hard to sort out. Rumors are spotty, stories don't jive, and corroboration is impossible. Even Draper's Web site (http://www. webcrunchers.com/crunch/) is more than a little hard to follow (this writer suspects he's protecting his inner circle). Here's what we do know.

Draper began sticking it to Ma Bell sometime around 1970 soon after he left the Air Force. Some say it all started when he met two blind kids, Jimmie and Dennie, somewhere around San Francisco. As one story goes, Dennie asked Draper for a long distance telephone number. The blind kid took Draper's number, but first dialed an 800 number. When the number began to ring, Dennie blew a tone from a plastic bosun's whistle that had been a free prize in a box of Cap'n Crunch Cereal. The tone from the whistle caused the ringing to stop. Jimmie, the other blind kid, used an electric organ to play a couple of chords into the receiver. The kid dialed Draper's number and magically the call was complete—and without those pesky long distance charges.

According to Draper's version, the blind kid Jimmie used notes played on an electric organ to produce the magic tones. Draper claims he heard about the Cap'n Crunch whistle (and another freebie whistle given away by the folks at Oscar Meyer) later in his hacking career. Maybe. But, to this day, plenty of phreakers believe that Draper discovered the secret of the Cap'n Crunch whistle while he was still in the Air Force.

Regardless of which legend you believe, Draper and the phreakers had uncovered a design flaw in the national telephone system (remember—these were the days before deregulation). To save money, the phone company transmitted voice traffic and the tones used to control switching over the same circuit. When one hole was glued shut, the Cap'n Crunch whistle emitted a perfect 2600hz cycle tone. Turns out the phone company used the very same 2600hz tone to switch a call to a long distance trunk line. In a pay phone, this sound was created when the proper amount of coins were inserted to complete a long distance call. This glitch changed Draper's life forever.

Draper began using the nickname Cap'n Crunch, and became cozy with a tight community of phone phreakers and hackers with names like Night Runner and Dr. Digital. It didn't take the group long to uncover more phone company secrets. One night Draper, a self-made electrical engineer, pulled out his parts box and slide rule. In about an hour he had constructed a contraption capable of generating the six basic tones used by the pre-digital phone system; 700hz, 900hz, 1100hz, 1300hz, 1500hz, and 1700hz. Draper's gizmo became known as the Blue Box. According to urban legend, Draper could be seen pulling up to a lonesome phone booth in his beat-up VW. He'd pull blow his Cap'n Crunch whistle into the receiver, and this would route his call to a long distance trunk. Then he'd use tones from his Blue Box to make the telephone company do his bidding. Legend has it Draper would spend hours, sometimes days, on these calls.

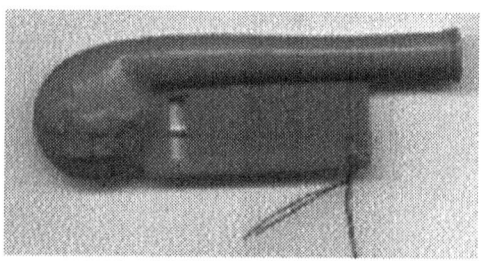

Cap'n Crunch Bosun Whistle
(From the author's Factoid collection)

At one point, Draper and his Blue Box scanned the 1-800 numbers assigned to the Washington D.C. exchange and came up with oodles of free lines to places like congressional offices and the White House. Phreakers also discovered that "flashing" the 2600hz tone to a busy 1-800 line would cause a three-way conversation. This is how operators interrupted a call in case of an emergency.

During one of his Washington forays, Draper and his friends discovered a 'special' 800 number. They flashed the line with the 2600hz tone, and eavesdropped on what they believed to be CIA gab. During one conversation, Draper overheard the code word 'Olympus'. The Phreakers had struck gold. Olympus was the code word used to summon the president of the United States to the phone.

The phreakers were ecstatic and hatched a plan. After creating a series of loop backs to cover their tracks, Draper and friends called the CIA number. A voice answered the call with "9337". One of Draper's buddies asked for Olympus. According to Draper, a voice sounding remarkably like Richard Nixon came on the line.

"What's going on?" asked the voice.

"We have a crisis here in Los Angeles," said the phreaker.

"What's the nature of the crisis?" said the Nixon voice.

"We're out of toilet paper, sir."

"Who is this," demanded the Nixon voice.

Draper ended the call.

The law doggies eventually caught up with Draper. He was arrested in 1972 after a series of grand jury investigations, and again in 1974. Cap'n Crunch did a short stint in the slammer where he wrote EasyWriter©, Apple's first word processor, and allegedly held phone-hacking workshops for fellow inmates. If you would like to catch up with Draper today, visit his Web site at http://www.webcrunchers.com/crunch/.

Addendum: While researching this story I ran across persistent rumors claiming Draper's discovery was nothing new. According to my sources, more than a few military servicemen knew about Ma Bell's long distance switching mechanisms. Many could reproduce the tone and get their long distance calls free of charge. This was known as the Navy Whistle.

978-0-595-31891-9
0-595-31891-6

www.ingramcontent.com/pod-product-compliance
Lightning Source LLC
Chambersburg PA
CBHW030750180526
45163CB00003B/961